ENDORSEMENTS

"This is the most compelling plea to restore preaching to its time-honored status that I have ever read. This book deserves to be read and reread to light the fire of passion and conviction for all who would publicly proclaim, 'Thus says the Lord.'"

—*Erwin Lutzer*
Senior Pastor, Moody Church
Chicago, Ill.

"This book combines the wisdom and experience of a number of the foremost preachers of the present day. If it is received as it ought to be, we may yet see a mighty change for good in the current spiritual scene. I hope it will be widely read."

—*Iain Murray*
Co-founder, Banner of Truth Trust
Edinburgh, Scotland

"*Feed My Sheep* is not only a passionate plea for preaching, but also a thorough review of what constitutes good preaching. Every minister of God's Word will profit from prayerfully reading this book."

—*Jerry Bridges*
author of *The Pursuit of Holiness*
Colorado Springs, Colo.

"Here some of this generation's most skilled shepherds provide passionate explanations of the priority and power of preaching God's Word so that it is a feast for Christ's sheep."

—*Bryan Chapell*
President, Covenant Theological Seminary
St. Louis, Mo.

"There are a lot of books on preaching today, but not many good ones—this one is good. The subjects covered (and the accents of the authors as well) commend this volume to the minister and seminary student—and, indeed, to the church member who wants to learn what a real preaching ministry looks like, and who wants that for his church and from his pastor. It is spiritually challenging and topically pertinent."

—*J. Ligon Duncan III*
Senior Minister, First Presbyterian Church
Jackson, Miss.

"There has never been a greater need for good preaching, and this book will help. In it some of the best preachers I know share their passion for preaching biblical, practical, expositional sermons that inform the mind and touch the heart. *Feed My Sheep* will be a tremendous help to anyone learning to preach and will provide real refreshment for anyone in the gospel ministry."

—*Philip Graham Ryken*
President, Wheaton College
Wheaton, Ill.

"When I was in seminary, my homiletics professor encouraged us to set a lifetime goal of reading at least one book each year on preaching. If you can read only one book this year on preaching, make it *Feed My Sheep*. Students and experienced preachers alike can find both timely and timeless teaching here. *Feed My Sheep* is simply one of the best books on preaching to come along in years."

—*Don Whitney*
author of *Spiritual Disciplines for the Christian Life*
Kansas City, Mo.

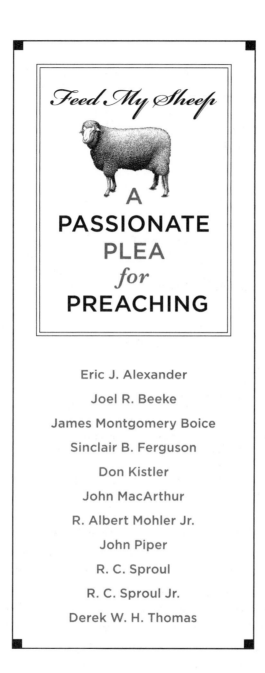

Feed My Sheep

A PASSIONATE PLEA *for* PREACHING

Eric J. Alexander

Joel R. Beeke

James Montgomery Boice

Sinclair B. Ferguson

Don Kistler

John MacArthur

R. Albert Mohler Jr.

John Piper

R. C. Sproul

R. C. Sproul Jr.

Derek W. H. Thomas

ℝ *Reformation Trust* A DIVISION OF LIGONIER MINISTRIES, ORLANDO, FL

Feed My Sheep: A Passionate Plea for Preaching

© 2008 by Ligonier Ministries

Previously published (2002) by Soli Deo Gloria Publications.

Published by Reformation Trust Publishing
a division of Ligonier Ministries
421 Ligonier Court, Sanford, FL 32771
Ligonier.org   ReformationTrust.com

Printed in Ann Arbor, Michigan
Sheridan Books, Inc.
January 2012
Second edition, second printing

Cover design: Dual Identity
Cover illustration: Michael Halbert
Interior design and typeset: Katherine Lloyd, The DESK

Unless otherwise indicated, all Scripture quotations in chapters 1, 8, 10, and 11 are from *The New American Standard Bible.*® Copyright © The Lockman Foundation 1960, 1962, 1963, 1968, 1971, 1972, 1973, 1975, 1995. Used by permission.

All Scripture quotations in chapters 2, 7, and 9 are from *The Holy Bible, New International Version*®. NIV®. Copyright © 1973, 1978, 1984 by International Bible Society. Used by permission of Zondervan. All rights reserved.

All Scripture quotations in chapters 3 and 6 are from *The Holy Bible, English Standard Version*, copyright © 2001 by Crossway Bibles, a division of Good News Publishers. Used by permission. All rights reserved.

All Scripture quotations in chapter 4 are from *The Holy Bible, King James Version.*

All Scripture quotations in chapter 5 are from *The New King James Version*®. Copyright © 1982 by Thomas Nelson. Used by permission. All rights reserved.

Scripture quotations marked RSV are from the *Revised Standard Version of the Bible*, Copyright © 1946, 1952, and 1971 National Council of the Churches of Christ in the United States of America. Used by permission. All rights reserved.

Library of Congress Cataloging-in-Publication Data
Feed my sheep : a passionate plea for preaching / R. Albert Mohler ... [et al.] ; foreword by J. Ligon Duncan III ; Don Kistler, general editor. -- [2nd ed.].
    p. cm.
  ISBN 978-1-56769-107-8
  1. Preaching. I. Mohler, R. Albert, 1959- II. Kistler, Don.
  BV4211.3.F44 2008
  251--dc22
                                                    2008027918

TABLE OF CONTENTS

FOREWORD

J. Ligon Duncan III

*T*he appearance of yet another book on preaching perhaps calls for some explanation. If the names on the title page are not sufficient in themselves to answer any query as to "why," I suggest the following: preaching in the contemporary English-speaking world—and even in the evangelical and Reformed community—has not been impervious to the negative forces brought to bear on proclamation as a method of evangelism and discipleship. A video-drowned and educationally-challenged culture, and a church bent on accommodating herself to the dominant communication theories of the day, challenge the minister committed to the "foolishness of preaching." He faces significant pressure to truncate and thin out his message, to entertain, to explore alternative media, and even to abandon historic modes of proclamation altogether. Such a milieu is discouraging in the extreme for the preacher (young or old, novice or master) who simply wants to be faithful. In this setting, every encouragement is useful. Indeed, it helps to beat this old drum and remind men that they are not crazy for wanting to remain faithful, to say to them, "Stay at the wheel; hold fast; keep on; don't give up; you're not alone." For this reason alone, this book may prove to be a real comfort and inducement to servants of the Word.

The subjects covered (and the accents of the authors) commend this volume to the minister and seminary student—and, indeed, to the church member who wants to learn what a real preaching ministry looks like, and who wants that for his church and from his pastor.

R. Albert Mohler Jr. dares to implore the overstretched, multi-tasking modern technician and spiritual therapist called a "pastor" to prioritize his ministry in such a way that the preaching of the Word becomes so central that everything else must fall into place behind it. Surely that is a timely exhortation, and a welcome, balancing emphasis to the siren calls of various lesser duties and congregational expectations.

James Boice helps buttress the preacher's resolve to stick with the "foolishness of preaching" in an age in which biblical authority is at a discount and congregations want their ears tickled instead of their hearts and minds challenged and instructed.

Derek Thomas's piece on expository preaching is a gem, one of the best short treatments of this issue you'll ever read. He bravely tips over some contemporary sacred cows and manages to advocate ably for the plan of consecutive, expositional preaching (that is, preaching verse by verse through books of the Bible)—surely a necessary emphasis in our time.

Joel R. Beeke makes a strong case for the classical Reformed view of ministerial piety and experiential preaching (a view which, it must be said, is out of step with many of the currents of present-day Reformed thought). A prayerful reading of this chapter may awaken us to the older, wiser counsel of our forefathers and bring a helpful corrective to the anti-experiential tendencies of our theological environment.

R. C. Sproul, in his usual engaging style, urges preachers to know the truth and teach it. He explores the possibilities of and problems in doing that, all the while drawing on the counsel of Martin Luther regarding the task of teaching the Word.

R. C. Sproul Jr. urges us to aim to preach the Word, and thus to preach to both the minds and hearts of our hearers. He also argues that while our preaching aspires to bring changed hearts and changed lives (under God's sovereignty, as His appointed means of grace), these are the fruits of changed minds. This nexus between our thinking and our living, also championed by the great Princeton theologians of the nineteenth century, is why the minister of the Word preaches to the mind and conscience of the hearer, and never bypasses the mind by a direct emotional appeal. Emotional experiences may be the product of truth worked deep into the soul, but the life emanates from the heart (which includes the mind and will in Bible thought), so that our thinking and desiring must be tapped if our living is ever to be right.

Sinclair Ferguson helpfully addresses the task of preaching to the heart. Reformed preachers aren't known for this in our day, but this was a hallmark of the older Reformed tradition, and Sinclair is himself a master of it. Lest one accidentally get the impression that this book's cry for substance in preaching is a call for arid conveyance of information, this chapter will put you right. (Of course, there are many calls for heart preaching throughout this book.)

Don Kistler urges men to preach with authority, citing examples of biblical preachers who did so, the greatest of whom was our Lord. This, too, is an important counterbalance to the chatty, self-effacing, tentative, informal, dialogical banter that sometimes passes for preaching today.

Eric Alexander, one of the archetypal Reformed preachers of our time, provides us with a Pauline perspective on evangelistic preaching (for those who still harbor suspicions that Reformed evangelistic preaching is an oxymoron!).

John Piper's timely treatment of preaching to those who are in the seminary of suffering (and that's all of us!) is simply brilliant. In his characteristic, God-exalting, grace-conveying manner, Piper deals with a subject of vital importance to the gospel ministry. There are broken hearts under our noses every time we preach, and that means we need a biblical grid for speaking to them. Piper gives this to us, while also helping us to respond appropriately to our own suffering

John MacArthur concludes the book by pointing us away from the messenger to the message preached, surely an important word of spiritual counsel in our success-focused and personality-centered culture. We are not the reason the gospel works; the gospel is the reason the gospel works.

This is a good book to read on preaching; it is spiritually challenging and topically pertinent. We find here an assemblage of veritable titans of robust evangelicalism, all of whom share in common a firm commitment to and ability for expository preaching (that is, the faithful explanation and application of the Bible in which the text of Scripture supplies the matter of the preacher's exhortations rather than the preacher using the text as an occasion for his own expostulations, however helpful those may be). The authors' topics are timely, their counsel is wise, and they will richly and quickly reward the teachable reader.

—J. Ligon Duncan III
Senior minister
First Presbyterian Church
Jackson, Miss.

PREFACE TO THE SECOND EDITION

*I*n the late 1990s, Don Kistler assembled an outstanding team of contributors to pour out their hearts on a crucial issue—preaching. The result was *Feed My Sheep*, one of the outstanding lay-level introductions to true evangelical preaching to be found today.

The book became one of the top sellers for Dr. Kistler's Soli Deo Gloria Publications, which was a tribute both to the men who graciously wrote chapters for the book and to Don's foresight in bringing the issue to the attention of Reformed believers.

When Soli Deo Gloria became part of Ligonier Ministries in 2004, demand for *Feed My Sheep* continued to be strong. Clearly interest in the subject matter remained high. Thus, when supplies of the paperback edition began to run low, it was an easy decision to reissue the book anew in a well-deserved hardback format.

Most of the authors of the various chapters in *Feed My Sheep* are pastors, and they often speak directly to their fellow ministers. This conversation is far from "shop talk," however. Every concerned layman can benefit from listening in as these gifted men discuss this vital topic.

It is our dual hope that this new edition of *Feed My Sheep* will help enflame a new generation of preachers to preach the Word and will educate a new generation of believers in the pew to understand what they ought to expect from the pulpit each Lord's Day.

—*The Publishers*
Reformation Trust

CONTRIBUTORS

Dr. R. Albert Mohler Jr. is the president of The Southern Baptist Theological Seminary in Louisville, Ky. He holds the M.Div. and PhD degrees from Southern Seminary. He is known for his insights into contemporary issues, which he discusses on two podcasts, *Thinking in Public* and *The Briefing*. He has appeared on such national television programs as *Larry King Live*, the *Today* show, and *Dateline NBC*. The *Chicago Tribune* has called him "an articulate voice for conservative Christianity at large." He is the author of several books, including *Culture Shift: Engaging Current Issues with Timeless Truth*; *Desire and Deceit: The Real Cost of the New Sexual Tolerance*; and *Atheism Remix: A Christian Confronts the New Atheists*, and has contributed to numerous other publications. Dr. Mohler is an ordained Southern Baptist minister and a member of the council of the Alliance of Confessing Evangelicals

Dr. James Montgomery Boice (1938–2000) was pastor of the Tenth Presbyterian Church in Philadelphia, Pa., for more than thirty-two years. He was a member of the International Council on Biblical Inerrancy and an editor for *Christianity Today*. Dr. Boice founded the Philadelphia Conference on Reformed Theology and had an extensive radio ministry through his *Bible Study Hour* program. His many books include commentaries on such biblical books as Genesis, Daniel, the Minor Prophets, John, Romans, Ephesians, and Philippians, as well as *Foundations of the Christian Faith* and *Whatever Happened to the Gospel of Grace? Rediscovering the Doctrines that Shook the World*.

Dr. Derek W. H. Thomas is an associate minister at First Presbyterian Church in Columbia, S.C., and an adjunct professor of systematic theology at Reformed Theological Seminary. He is a council member of the Alliance of Confessing Evangelicals, which he also serves as editorial director and as editor in chief of *Reformation21*, the Alliance's online magazine. A native of Wales, Dr. Thomas graduated from RTS in 1978, then pastored for seventeen years in Belfast,

Northern Ireland. He earned his PhD from the University of Wales, Lampeter. He served as the minister of teaching at First Presbyterian Church in Jackson, Miss., before his call to Columbia. He has written numerous books, including *The Storm Breaks: Job Simply Explained*; *Wisdom: The Key to Living God's Way*; and *How the Gospel Brings Us All the Way Home*. He also co-edited *Give Praise to God: A Vision for Reforming Worship*.

Dr. Joel R. Beeke is president and professor of systematic theology and homiletics at Puritan Reformed Theological Seminary; a pastor of the Heritage Netherlands Reformed Congregation; editor of *Banner of Sovereign Grace Truth*; editorial director of Reformation Heritage Books; president of Inheritance Publishers; and vice president of the Dutch Reformed Translation Society, all in Grand Rapids, Mich. He has written, coauthored, or edited some fifty books (most recently, *Meet the Puritans*, *Living for God's Glory: An Introduction to Calvinism*, *Parenting by God's Promises*, and *Heirs with Christ: The Puritans on Adoption*) and contributed hundreds of articles to Reformed books, journals, periodicals, and encyclopedias. His PhD is in Reformation and post-Reformation theology from Westminster Theological Seminary. He is frequently called on to lecture at seminaries and to speak at Reformed conferences around the world.

Dr. R. C. Sproul is the founder and chairman of Ligonier Ministries in Orlando, Fla., and president of the Ligonier Academy of Biblical and Theological Studies. He serves as minister of preaching and teaching at Saint Andrew's, a Reformed congregation in Sanford, Fla. His teaching is heard on the daily radio program *Renewing Your Mind*. He has taught at several seminaries around the United States and is in constant demand as a speaker at conferences. Dr. Sproul has written more than seventy books, among them *The Holiness of God, Chosen by God, Abortion: A Rational Look at an Emotional Issue, A Taste of Heaven: Worship in the Light of Eternity*, and *The Truth of the Cross*. He also served as general editor of *The Reformation Study Bible*.

Dr. R. C. Sproul Jr. is a teaching fellow of Ligonier Ministries and an assistant professor of theology, philosophy, and apologetics at Reformation Bible College at Ligonier Academy in Sanford, Fla. He planted Saint Peter Presbyterian Church in Southwest Virginia and is the founder, chairman, and teacher of Highlands Ministries. He holds degrees from Grove City College, Reformed Theological Seminary, and Whitefield Theological Seminary. Dr. Sproul is the author or editor of a dozen books, the most recent of which are *Believing God: 12 Biblical Promises Christians Struggle to Accept; After Darkness, Light: Essays in Honor of R. C. Sproul;* and *When You Rise Up: A Covenantal Approach to Homeschooling.* He is a regular columnist for *Tabletalk* and *Homeschooling Today* magazines, and a frequent conference speaker.

Dr. Sinclair B. Ferguson is senior minister of the historic First Presbyterian Church in Columbia, S.C., and a professor of systematic theology at Redeemer Theological Seminary in Dallas, Texas. A native of Scotland, Dr. Ferguson earned three degrees, including his PhD, from the University of Aberdeen. He was ordained into the ministry in the Church of Scotland and spent some sixteen years in ministry in his homeland, including five years at St. George's-Tron Church in Glasgow. He has been an editor and a trustee with the Banner of Truth Trust publishing house and is a prolific author. His published titles include *The Holy Spirit, Grow in Grace, Let's Study Philippians, John Owen on the Christian Life, In Christ Alone: Living the Gospel-Centered Life, By Grace Alone: How the Grace of God Amazes Me,* and, for children, *The Big Book of Questions & Answers* and *The Big Book of Questions & Answers About Jesus.* Dr. Ferguson is a member of the council of the Alliance of Confessing Evangelicals and a teaching fellow with Ligonier Ministries.

Dr. Don Kistler is a Bible teacher, author, and editor. He founded Soli Deo Gloria Publications, which published hundreds of classic Puritan titles, and now heads The Northampton Press. Dr. Kistler holds the M.Div. from Luther Rice Seminary and the D.Min. from Whitefield Theological Seminary, and is an ordained minister. Prior to entering the gospel ministry, Dr. Kistler coached high school and college football for more than fifteen years. He is the author of the books A *Spectacle Unto God: The Life and Death of Christopher Love,* and *Why Read the Puritans Today?* and has contributed to numerous other books.

Eric J. Alexander is a retired pastor of St. George's-Tron Church in Glasgow, Scotland, and a council member of the Alliance of Confessing Evangelicals. He is a former president of the Universities and Colleges Christian Fellowship (UCCF) in Great Britain, and he served as chairman of the Scottish Council of the Overseas Missionary Fellowship. Rev. Alexander preaches and teaches at conferences and seminaries in Europe and the United States.

Dr. John Piper is pastor for preaching and vision at the Bethlehem Baptist Church in Minneapolis, Minn., and chancellor of Bethlehem College and Seminary. He holds the B.Div. degree from Fuller Theological Seminary and a doctorate from the University of Munich. He taught biblical studies at Bethel College for six years before accepting his pastorate. Dr. Piper is known through his Desiring God Ministries. He is the author of *Desiring God: Meditations of a Christian Hedonist*; *The Pleasures of God*; *Let the Nations Be Glad! The Supremacy of God in Missions*; *God's Passion for His Glory: Living the Vision of Jonathan Edwards*; *Don't Waste Your Life*; *What Jesus Demands of the World*; *The Future of Justification*; and many more books.

Dr. John MacArthur has served as pastor-teacher of Grace Community Church in Sun Valley, Calif., for forty years and is heard on more than two thousand radio outlets worldwide on the radio program *Grace to You*. He is president of The Master's College and Seminary and has written numerous books, including *Charismatic Chaos*, *Faith Works*, *The Gospel According to Jesus*, *Ashamed of the Gospel*, *A Tale of Two Sons*, and *The Truth War*. He is also the author of the twenty-six-volume MacArthur New Testament Commentary series. He travels widely as a conference speaker.

Chapter 1

THE PRIMACY OF PREACHING

R. Albert Mohler Jr.

*E*vangelical pastors commonly state that biblical preaching is the hallmark of their calling. Nevertheless, a careful observer might come to a very different conclusion. The priority of preaching is simply not evident in far too many churches.

We must affirm with Martin Luther that the preaching of the Word is the first essential mark of the church. Luther believed so strongly in the centrality of preaching that he stated, "Now, wherever you hear or see this Word preached, believed, professed, and lived, do not doubt that the true *ecclesia sancta catholica* [Christian, holy people] must be there. . . . And even if there were no other sign than this alone, it would still suffice to prove that a Christian, holy people must exist there, for God's Word cannot be without God's people and, conversely, God's people cannot be without God's Word."[1]

A Servant of the Word

The preacher is called to be a servant of the Word. That statement is an expression of a very proud and glorious lineage in Christian history. But it was made particularly well-known among preachers in 1941, when H. H. Farmer delivered a series of addresses on preaching and then published them under the title *The Servant of the Word*.[2]

Farmer represented the neoorthodox recovery of preaching. After a period of theological and homiletical sterility, figures such as Farmer in England, Karl Barth in Switzerland, and others in the English-speaking world and in greater Europe sought to reassert the case for preaching. In *The Servant of the Word*, Farmer had a great deal to say about preaching; he argued for the affirmation of the Christian message through the continuation of preaching in the church. But despite his book's title, Farmer actually had very little to say about the Word. As a result, this neoorthodox argument for preaching was a house built on theological sand—it did not last.

Such an argument for preaching was made necessary by the assertion, which was widespread at the time, that preaching was outmoded as a form of Christian communication. It was seen as something the church could do without. Farmer maintained, however, that the practice of preaching was indispensable to Christianity.

Farmer got a number of things right. First, he argued for the unique power and preeminence of preaching in Christianity. The history-of-religion approach was very influential at that time. This school of thought held that preaching was part of virtually every religious system in one way or another. Farmer maintained, however, that such a claim simply was not honest. Preaching has a priority among Christians that it does not have in other faith traditions, and this is because of the very nature of the gospel.

Second, Farmer argued that the unique authority of Christian preaching comes from the authority of revelation and, in particular, the Bible. Contrary to those who maintained that revelation was basically internal, emotional, and relational, Farmer argued that it was external, historical, and given. He stated:

> For Christianity is a religion of revelation; its central message is a declaration, a proclamation that God has met the darkness of the human spirit with a great unveiling of succoring light and truth. The revelation moreover is historical, that is to say, it is given primarily through events which in the first place can only be reported and affirmed. As we have already said, no merely internal reflection can arrive at historical events. If a man is to be saved, he must be confronted again and again with the givenness of Christ.[3]

This is an interesting statement. In it, we discover an argument that Christian preaching is distinguished by virtue of its grounding in revelation. It is the preaching of a God-given Word, not a human message (2 Peter 1:16)

My concern, of course, is not with what *H. H. Farmer* thought about the preacher as the servant of the Word. I want an apostolic authority, one inspired by the Holy Spirit, namely, the apostle Paul. I am concerned to discover what the great apostle thought about preaching and how he understood *himself* to be the servant of the Word. To make this discovery, I want to examine a portion of Paul's letter to the Colossians:

> Of this church I was made a minister according to the stewardship from God bestowed on me for your benefit, so that I might fully carry out the preaching of the Word of God, that is, the mystery which has been hidden from the past ages and generations, but now has been manifested to His saints, to whom God willed to make known what is the riches of the glory of this mystery among the Gentiles, which is Christ in you, the hope of glory. We proclaim Him, admonishing every man and teaching every man with all wisdom, so that we might present every man complete in Christ. For this purpose also I labor, striving according to His power, which mightily works within me. (Col. 1:25–29)[4]

This is a majestic passage. Paul writes here of his understanding of the apostolic ministry, of his stewardship of the mysteries of God, and of his task of proclaiming the Word of God. He speaks of his calling, his message, and the purpose of his preaching. This is Paul's declaration of his ministry: he sees himself as a servant of the Word.

We must notice what goes before this passage: "Now I rejoice in my sufferings for your sake, and in my flesh I do my share on behalf of His body, which is the church, in filling up what is lacking in Christ's afflictions" (v. 24). Here Paul states that he not only endures suffering but, of all things, rejoices in it. Why? The passage that follows gives the explanation, and it is gloriously counterintuitive. He rejoices in his sufferings because they have earned him the opportunity to preach the gospel. Paul sees his purpose on earth as preaching this Word and proclaiming Jesus Christ.

This passage, then, does not represent superficial triumphalism, but genuine gospel triumph. It is a sober triumph, because Paul acknowledges the sufferings he is enduring, but he also understands the victory that is assured in Christ. It is not Paul's triumph. It is Christ in Paul, the hope of glory.

Hidden Results, Frequent Controversies

In contrast, we see the exhaustion of preaching that has taken place in so many pulpits in the contemporary church. Rarely do we hear these days that a church is distinguished primarily by its preaching. When we hear people speak about their own congregations or make comparative remarks about other congregations, generally they speak about something other than preaching. They might speak of a church's "ministry." They might speak of specialized programs for senior adults, children, or young people. They might speak of a church's music. Sometimes they might speak of things far more superficial. Or perhaps they speak of the church's Great Commission vigor and commitment—and for that we are certainly thankful. But rarely do you hear a church described, first and foremost, by the character, power, and content of its preaching. This is because few preachers today are true servants of the Word.

I acknowledge that pastors have a certain "product envy." We envy those who build houses or sell cars or build great corporations or assemble automobiles. Why? It is because they have something tangible to show for their labor at the end of the day. They may be assembling widgets. They may be putting things in boxes, sealing them up, and sending them out. They may be cutting the grass. But in each case, they can see the product of their hands. A carpenter or an artist or a building contractor has something to which he can point.

But what about the preacher? The preacher is denied that satisfaction. We are not given the sight to see what we would like to see. It seems as if we stand up and throw out words and wonder what becomes of them. What, after all, is our product? Words, words, and more words. We sometimes feel as if we are flattering ourselves that people even remember what it was we had to say. We are chastened from even asking our own church members and fellow believers to recall our text halfway through the next week. Why? Because we are afraid that we will get that shocked look of anticipated response when a person of good intentions simply says: "That was a fine message. I don't remember exactly what it was about, and I have a very vague recollection of something you may have said, but I want you to know it was powerful."

Paul responds to this, at least in part, in verse 23, when he writes, "[All of this is true,] if indeed, you continue in the faith firmly established and steadfast, and not moved away from the hope of the gospel that you have heard, which was proclaimed in all creation under heaven and of which I, Paul, was made a minister." Paul understood that it was possible to hear in vain, and he hoped that it was not true of the Colossian church, that their response to his preaching was not just a succession of nice accolades and respectful comments.

Wouldn't we like to have an assembly line of maturing Christians going out the door of the church, wherein we could at least see something and note some progress? Perhaps we could even statistically mark what kind of impact one sermon had over against another. But we do not have that sight; the pulpit ministry is largely a hidden work in the human heart. Such a work will bear good fruit, but it will take time to show.

Since the Lord established His church, there have been preachers—lots of preachers. The church has heard good preachers and poor preachers, faithful preachers and faithless preachers, eloquent preachers and pulpit babblers, pulpit humorists and pulpit bawlers, expository preachers, narrative preachers, thematic preachers, evangelistic preachers, literary preachers, sawdust preachers, postmodern preachers, seeker-sensitive preachers, famous preachers, infamous preachers—lots and lots of preachers. Accumulated, their work amounts to many millions of hours of preaching.

This represents a massive investment of human time, energy, and attention in the task of preaching, as well as countless books, conferences, and controversies. So what? The preacher may sound like Luther on Sunday, but he feels like bathing in Ecclesiastes on Monday morning: "Vanity, vanity, all is vanity." Preaching can seem like striving after the wind. We feel like the preacher of Ecclesiastes, who laments in 1:15, "What is crooked cannot be straightened and what is lacking cannot be counted." Vanity. Such is life for those who are called to preach: Hard work with (often) no tangible, positive result.

Furthermore, this line of work has a nasty way of getting you into trouble. It seems that the more faithful one is in preaching, the more trouble one encounters.

Why? You did not come up with the Word. This is not your opinion. It is not something you are saying in order to offend people. You are simply preaching it. After all, that is your assignment. So you preach the truth, and the next thing you know you are on the front page of the papers. You are the subject of gossip for the deacons and their wives; even the youth group is up in arms over what you said. Conflict and controversy are always hard, and they tend to be correlated to faithfulness in preaching. The harder you work at it, the greater the risk.

Sometimes it happens that preaching the Word is met with antipathy and resistance. Why? Because "the word of God is living and active and sharper than any two-edged sword" (Heb. 4:12a). And as the Lord spoke to His prophet Isaiah, "[My Word] will not return to Me empty, without accomplishing what I desire" (55:11b). Sometimes this means that God uses the Word to rebuke and correct His people. And it is the preacher who must speak that word and reap the response. Sometimes preachers are ejected and fired. That is simply one of the realities of pulpit ministry.

And it is not just conflict and controversy. Sometimes, preachers experience persecution or even martyrdom. The man who wrote the letter to the Colossians was himself to be a martyr for the faith. In giving his final instructions to Timothy, he speaks of being poured out as a libation. He is ready to be offered as an offering. The sufferings of which he speaks in Colossians 1:24 are going to be realized in a martyrdom that is yet before him. There have been martyrs throughout the history of the church, but the blood of those martyrs has been the seed of the church, nourishing its growth.

Do you not imagine that your preaching priorities would become clear under persecution? After all, if you are forced to meet with your congregation in a catacomb, and if you know that you might be arrested at any time, you are going to weigh every word. There is not going to be any time for pulpit frivolity. There is not going to be any time to promote the next youth program. You are going to be concerned with getting down to the reality of the eternal Word of God.

Indeed, I will go so far as to assert that if you are at peace with the world, you have abdicated your calling. You have become a court preacher to some earthly power, no matter how innocuous it may appear. To put it straight: you have been bought! If there is no controversy in your ministry, there is probably very little content to your preaching. The content of the Word of God is not only alive and active, it is sharper than any two-edged sword, and that means it does some surgery. Cutting leads to bleeding, and by God's grace healing then comes, but there is *always* controversy.

Paul is emphatically aware of this dynamic. He understands the reality of preaching. He understands the frustration, and he sometimes articulates it in his own words. Just read his letters. It is not as if he avoided controversy. In 1 Corinthians 1:14, he lays it right before them, even to the point of saying, "I thank God that I baptized none of you except Crispus and Gaius." That's a rather strong word of rebuke. But this text hits us where we need it, because Paul not only endures all of this, he seems to revel in it, to celebrate it. Paul seems to understand all of the frustrations, the conflict, the controversy, and the trouble of preaching, and yet he says, as it were: "Bring it on. This is what I was made for. This is what I was called to do. This is what I am here for. Let's get at it!"

In Colossians 1:24, Paul even rejoices in his sufferings for the sake of the church, for the body of Christ and for His glory. "Of this church," Paul says, "I was made a minister. I was not made a minister of some hypothetical, non-problematic, non-controversial church. I was made a minister of the church of the Lord Jesus Christ, of the body of Christ on earth, a chosen, purchased possession being sanctified even in the present, and struggling against the powers of sin and death and evil and darkness."

The Chief Priority of Ministry

Then Paul makes the point in verse 25 that the central purpose of ministry is the preaching of the Word. In the end, everything comes down to this. "Of this church, I was made a minister according to the stewardship from God bestowed on me for your benefit, so that I might fully carry out *the preaching of the Word of God*" (emphasis added). The words "the preaching of" are not in the original language, but are inserted in some translations, and I believe that is a legitimate insertion. It is clear that what Paul means is that the ministry of the Word of God is achieved by the proclamation, the teaching, and the preaching of the Word of God.

Paul speaks in very strong language. He speaks of the fact that he was *made* a minister. He did not make himself a minister anymore than he saved himself or appeared to himself on the Damascus Road. He was claimed, and as he was claimed, he was made a minister of the Word. In fact, he was made an apostle of the Lord Jesus Christ, and he understood his situation clearly. In 1 Corinthians 15:8, he explains that Christ appeared to him as "one untimely born." He called himself the "least of the apostles" in verse 9, because he had persecuted the church. But God's great triumphant sign was His choice of the chief persecutor of the church to be the apostle to the Gentiles.

Paul goes on to say that he *received* this ministry according to the stewardship from God bestowed on him for the benefit of the Colossian church. I think this is critical to the pastor's understanding of his calling and stewardship. We have a stewardship from God that is bestowed on us, not for our benefit but for the benefit of the church. It is as if we have been drafted, called out, assigned, and granted a stewardship that we do not deserve and are not capable of fulfilling. Nonetheless, God chooses such instruments. In 1 Corinthians 1:20, 27–28, Paul wrote:

> Where is the wise man? Where is the scribe? Where is the debater of this age? Has not God made foolish the wisdom of the world? . . . God has chosen the foolish things of the world to shame the wise, and God has chosen the weak things of the world to shame the things which are strong, and the base things of the world and the despised God has chosen, the things that are not, so that He may nullify the things that are.

Why has God done these things? So that there may be no boasting except in God.

"We are stewards of the mysteries of God," Paul says, according to the stewardship God bestowed on him "for the benefit of the church." Why? What is the bottom line? What is the essential point? The point, as you can see in the purpose clause of Colossians 1:25, is, "so that I might fully carry out the preaching of the Word of God." Paul's intention was not to dabble a little bit in preaching; nor was it his intention merely to add preaching to his ministerial resume or itinerary in order that he might complete himself as a well-rounded minister of the gospel. Neither was it that he would eventually get around to preaching in the midst of other pastoral responsibilities. No, he said, "All of this, in the end, is fulfilled, and is only fulfilled, in fully carrying out my responsibility of preaching the Word."

When the minister of the gospel faces the Lord God as judge, there will be many questions addressed to him. There will be many standards of accountability. There will be many criteria of judgment. But in the end, the most essential criterion of judgment for the minister of God is, "Did you preach the Word? Did you fully carry out the ministry of the Word? In season and out of season, was the priority of your ministry the preaching of the Word?"

This is not to say that there are not other responsibilities or that there are not even other priorities for a pastor. However, there is one central, non-negotiable, immovable, essential priority, and that is the preaching of the Word of God. And Paul speaks to this so clearly when he states his purpose: "That I might fully carry out the preaching of the Word of God."

Contrast the absolute priority of preaching in Paul's ministry with the frequent confusion in today's congregations. What we see is the marginalization of the pulpit. Some would tell us, "Preaching has its place, but let's not let preaching get in the way of music, which is, after all, what draws people, and what establishes fellowship." Perhaps many of us could testify of going to a church service where something was said or even printed in the bulletin to the effect that "first we are going to have a time of worship and then we are going to turn to preaching." What do we think preaching is? It is the central act of Christian worship! As a matter of fact, everything else ought to build to the preaching of the Word, for that is when the God of whom we have been speaking and singing speaks to us from His eternal and perfect Word.

When we look at manuals, books, magazines, seminars, and conferences addressed to pastors, we notice that preaching, if included at all, is most often not the priority. When we hear people speak about how to grow a church and build a great congregation, few and far between are those who say it comes essentially by the preaching of the Word. We know why this is so. It is because growth comes by the preaching of the Word *slowly*, immeasurably, sometimes even invisibly. Hence we are back to the problem mentioned above. If you want to see quick results, the preaching of the Word just might not be the way to go. If you are going to define results in terms of statistics, numbers, and visible response, it just might be that there are other mechanisms, other programs, and other means that will produce that faster. The question is whether other methods produce Christians.

Indeed, such techniques will *not* produce maturing and faithful believers in the Lord Jesus Christ. Only the preaching of the Word yields that sort of fruit. Preaching is not a mechanism for communication that was developed by preachers who needed something to do on Sunday. It was not some kind of sociological or technological adaptation by the church in the first century in an effort to come up with something to fill the time between the invocation and benediction. It was the central task of preaching that framed not only their understanding of worship, but also their understanding of the church. And so it ought to be today.

Luther tried to go back to the first century and understand the essential marks of the church, and the first mark he listed was preaching. Where the authentic preaching of the Word takes place, the church is there, he said. By contrast, where it is absent, there is no church. No matter how high the steeple, no matter how large the budget, no matter how impressive the ministry, it is something other than the church.

Paul was fully determined to carry out his ministry of preaching the Word of God, and he did so in the face of the tyranny of the practical, the immediate, and the seemingly productive, because his confidence, after all, was in the Word of God.

The Content of Preaching

The essential content of Christian preaching, Paul says, is the mystery of the gospel. He writes that the preaching of the Word of God is seen in "the mystery which has been hidden from the past ages and generations, but has now been manifested to His saints" (Col. 1:26). A mystery? All around Asia Minor and the ancient world at this time, there were mystery religions and mystery cults, and there were some who thought, especially from the Roman perspective, that Christianity was just another one of them. After all, it had its mystery. And Paul said, "Guilty as charged." Yet this is not a mystery of esoteric knowledge. This is not a gnosticism of elitist intellectuals. No, this is a mystery that was hidden by God until it could be publicly revealed in the incarnation of Jesus Christ, in His death, burial, and resurrection. This is a mystery!

There is something deeply mysterious about Christian preaching, both in terms of its communication and in terms of its content. After all, what we preach is not what the world expects to hear. It is not a message they will hear anywhere else. No human wisdom, no school of philosophy, no secular salesman, no TV commercial speaker selling his CDs is ever going to come up with this on his own. Take a look at what is selling in the bookstores and who is hosting the big conferences. You'll realize that if you can tell people how to buy property and profit from its renovation, you can sell your messages. If you can tell people how to lose weight, you can sell just about anything. If you can tell people how to become handsome and wise, raise children who are well-behaved, and have their pets like them, you will find yourself to be a very popular speaker. You could put your DVDs and CDs together and write books that would be sold in bookstores and hawked on television.

But if you preach the gospel, you just might discover that it is not quite so popular. But it is powerful and it is mysterious. Why? Because it was a mystery that God hid from previous generations in order that it might be displayed publicly at the time of the Lord Jesus Christ.

Look at Paul's statement in verses 26–27: "that is, the mystery which has been hidden from past ages and generations, but has now been manifested to His saints, to whom God willed to make known what is the riches of the glory of this mystery among the Gentiles, which is Christ in you, the hope of glory." As Paul quite personally knew, true preaching often leads to a riot. But the true preaching of the gospel is the preaching of the mystery of God. It was hidden, but now it is revealed to the Gentiles. The Gentiles had been understanding God's way about as correctly as someone using a Ouija board. But out of that darkness, out of that confusion, out of that sinful depravity, out of that backwardness, and out of that ignorance had come the shining light of the gospel, which is a mystery. It is the mystery of mysteries: Christ in us, the hope of glory.

There is glory, and this glory can even come to us, but it is not ours. There is a glory we should seek, but it is not glory for ourselves, but the glory of Christ. And that glory is most evident not just when Christ is preached as an abstract and objective truth, but when Christ becomes in us the hope of glory. Paul's concern was not just that his hearers would come to a correct cognitive understanding of the gospel, although that was essential. His concern was that the gospel would be received by faith and that lives would be transformed. Paul's wonderfully symphonic presentation of the gospel in the book of Romans helps us to understand how sinners become saints, how we are justified by faith, and how we are adopted as sons and daughters of the Most High God.

Paul understood this to be a mystery. And if it is a mystery for the Jews, it is even more a mystery for the Gentiles. Indeed, in those central passages in Romans, Paul helps to explain how it is that the branch of the wild olive tree has been grafted onto Israel. It is a mystery, and if you do not get excited about preaching this, I'm not sure what will excite you! The gospel is simply the most transformative, the most powerful, and the most explosive message there is. If you have a problem finding something to preach, I guarantee that you are not preaching the gospel.

The gospel, according to Paul, is not simply offered to us on a platter for our convenience, our investigation, or our tasting. It is thrown at us like hot, blazing rocks spewed forth from the crater of a volcano. It is uniquely dangerous. Our task is to preach the Word and to make known the mystery.

Making known the mystery requires diligence—painstaking, systematic, rigorous, expository preaching. Why? Because we have to paint the entire canvas. Too many preachers are working out of one little corner of the great canvas of the work of God. There are some preachers who, as painters, only have certain colors. Some have the vivid colors. Some have the subdued colors. But in order to get the entire picture out there, what is required is rigorous expository preaching, because we have to connect the dots.

Painting the whole picture requires that we go into the Old and New Testaments, and we have to use the analogy of faith, that is, the analogy of Scripture, to interpret and apply Scripture by Scripture. We have to build upon knowledge so that the people of God are continually increasing in the knowledge of the Word of God, and so that the Word of God is taking root in them and growing in them. Only then will they begin to see the whole picture. They will understand its component parts. They'll understand the bright colors and the subdued hues. Indeed, they will understand the gospel. The mystery will come into focus.

That is the power of preaching. Focus will not come by any other means. Sadly, however, the doctrinal ignorance in the pulpits of today is being replicated in the doctrinal ignorance and indifference of the pews, and the people are not even seeing the picture, much less getting it.

The Goal of Preaching

What does it mean to be a servant of the Word? It means that the promise of true preaching is to present every Christian complete in Christ. Paul says this in verse 28: "We proclaim Him, admonishing every man and teaching every man with all wisdom, so that we may present every man complete in Christ." How about that for a job description? What a challenge!

Note again what Paul says here: "We proclaim *Him*." We preach Christ; we proclaim Him; we focus our message on Christ. We show Christ, the mystery of the ages, revealed in Scripture in the Old Testament and in the New. We proclaim Him at every opportunity and from every text. The best exhortation I know concerning this practice comes from the great Baptist preacher Charles Haddon Spurgeon, who, in speaking to his students about expository preaching, told them to preach a particular text and, as soon as possible, make a beeline to the cross and show its fulfillment in Jesus Christ.

In addition to proclaiming Christ, Paul says we are to admonish every man. This issue of admonishing is undervalued in our day, as exemplified by the precious little admonishment we hear in our pulpits. Paul, however, believed in admonishing. In fact, he described his ministry in many ways as admonishing. He even spoke of his ministry to the Ephesians as years of admonishment (Acts 20:31).

What does it mean to admonish? For one thing, it means to get in the face. These days, with our ideals of personal autonomy and personal privacy, we Americans feel that no one has the right to tell us what to believe, how to act, or what is correct in terms of behavior or patterns of thought and life. After all, we reason, "Our marriages are our marriages. We are free to make and to break them. Our vocations are between us and our employers. Our lives are our own. God does not have anything to do with them, and the church certainly better not stick its nose into them." In our day, this would be seen as an intolerant and invasive imposition. Indeed, it would be seen as arrogant.

That is hardly the pattern in the New Testament. Under a ministry of authentic

Christian preaching, the Word is applied. I do not mean that it is applied in the sense that the preacher tries to find some way to make the text relevant. Rather, it is applied in that the text is directly addressed to persons in the congregation: "This is what you must do. This is what you must be."

Isaac Backus, the great Baptist, was an exhorter before he was a preacher. In revolutionary America, the exhorter had a particular task in the congregation, and it was not one that was likely to be popular. After the preacher had preached, it was his responsibility to apply the message. This might mean going up to somebody and saying, "This is going to be how you change your behavior." Backus was 15 years old when he took on this assignment. He would come up after the preaching and say, "Now, Widow Jones, this means you are going to have to change the way you raise your children." Or, "Mr. Smith, this means you are going to have to change the way you do your business." We have to be accountable to the Word of God, and we have to be accountable together.

Whether from the preacher or the believer in the pew, there simply is not much admonishment going on in today's church. But the role of the preacher is to expose error and to reveal sin. The Word of God will do that, I promise you, as you preach the Word. It is simply there in the text. So we have to come into alignment with this text in terms of the way we think, the way we worship, and the way we live, or we are going to disobey. Those are the only options.

In 2 Timothy 3:16–17, Paul told Timothy that in the preaching of the Word he was to rebuke and to correct. Correcting is not very politically correct. Why? Because you have to say that someone is wrong, that someone's particular understanding needs to be brought into alignment with God's Word. It means a behavior needs to be rebuked. Sadly, the general absence of church discipline in our age has often made the church just another volunteer association, except with a steeple.

Finally, Paul says that in addition to proclaiming Christ and admonishing every man, we must teach every man, specifically, the positive teaching of the Word of God with application. This is something that cannot be sequestered to Sunday school. We cannot assume that the teaching ministry of the church is fulfilled when we have a good children's education system. The teaching of the Word of God should be cross-generational. It is to be progressive and accumulative, thereby growing saints toward maturity in the Lord Jesus Christ.

Furthermore, the teaching of the Word of God is to comfort, and it should do so, foremost, from the pulpit, for the pastor is, of all things, the teacher of the church.

The Authority of Preaching

Teaching assumes authority. After all, we have to know what it is we are to teach. Far too many preachers think this is an authority that is personal. "It is my authority, for I am the one who has been elected to teach," or so the thought often goes. Others think that it is the authority of modern knowledge they bring in or the authority of secular consensus that is needed. But there is only one authority that undergirds and justifies the preacher's teaching ministry, and that is the authority of the Word of God. This Word is inerrant, infallible, authoritative, and trustworthy. It is not only the foundation, but the substance, the content of our teaching and preaching. In too many churches today there is an uncertain sound from the pulpit, a multiple-choice curriculum of doctrine being offered. We have our own version of "values clarification," but that is not the model of the apostle Paul. It was not his understanding of his stewardship and it is not the nature of our calling.

The awesome power of authentic preaching is seen in the fact that God uses preaching to present His saints complete in Christ. How are Christians to grow? How are they to be matured? How is the process of Holy Spirit-directed sanctification to be seen in them? It happens by the preaching of the Word.

The fruit of the preaching of the Word will be made visible. Our product envy will be very temporary. For when we get to glory, we will see the product of our preaching. We will see saints clothed in the righteousness of Christ. We will see men and women, brothers and sisters in Christ, made complete in Him. When we measure whether or not we are successful, it must be by this criterion, namely, are we seeing the saints growing to completeness in Jesus Christ?

Paul concludes by stating in verse 29 that it is for this purpose that he struggles, a struggle not in his own strength, but according to Christ's power which works mightily within us. The apostle knew that he was not up to this, but Christ was. Paul's authority was nothing, but Christ was all-sufficient, as revealed in His Word. This means we have to devote ourselves to preaching not as one priority among others, but as our central and highest priority.

Faithful Servants of the Word

What does it mean to be a servant of the Word? First, if we are to be servants of the Word, the priorities of our ministry must be such that the preaching of the Word is central—*everything else* must fall into place behind this priority. Are there other important tasks of ministry? Of course. Are there other important priorities of the church? Of course. But your personal schedule must reflect the priority of preaching, showing just how serious you are about it. You can find out quickly what a church believes about preaching by looking at its calendar for worship and other activities, and you can find out what a preacher believes about preaching by looking at his schedule. Every other task and priority must be subordinated to that first priority, the preaching of the Word—with the promise that it will balance all the others. Everything comes into proper balance because we do not have to worry about balancing a schedule, balancing a budget, or balancing priorities when we understand that the Word of God will establish those priorities. Then everything else will become clear.

Second, our congregations must be aware of this priority and honor it. The congregation needs to understand that preaching is not merely the preacher's responsibility. It is the congregation's responsibility to see that it is fed, so it is the congregation's responsibility to call a preacher who will preach the Word. Then it is the congregation's responsibility to hold him accountable for that preaching and to measure his effectiveness and his faithfulness to, of all things, the pulpit ministry.

Third, if we are to be servants of the Word, our preaching must be truly expository. That is, it must truly expound and apply the text of Scripture, declaring the Word of God to the people of God with admonishment, then trusting the Holy Spirit to apply that Word. Preaching the Word of God takes rigorous exposition—by which I do not mean just choosing the texts we like, the texts we think will preach, or the texts that will fall on all the right ears, but the text as it stands. I believe in verse-by-verse exposition, because otherwise we would never get to some of those challenging texts that are just so difficult to preach. But they, too, are the inerrant, infallible, and authoritative Word of God. They are profitable for our preaching and for our teaching, and how we deal with them is a measure of our stewardship. As noted above, this kind of preaching can get a man into serious trouble, and the lack of trouble ought to be a signal that, perhaps, this kind of preaching is not found in his pulpit.

In the final analysis, we will know how faithful we have been only in glory. When we see our Savior face to face, and when we see all the saints to whom we have preached, we will discover whether or not our preaching contributed to their completeness in Christ. Paul said that all of the suffering, the diligence, the hard work, the controversy, and the martyrdom was for the glory of preaching the gospel. And he said the purpose behind it was to see every man, every Christian, perfected in Christ and presented to our Lord and Savior. Failure at this task is simply too awful to contemplate.

Endnotes

[1] Martin Luther, "On the Councils and the Church," in Luther's *Works* [*LW*], ed. Jaroslav Pelikan (vols. 1–30) and Helmut T. Lehmann (vols. 31–55), vol. 41, *Church and Ministry III*, ed. Eric W. Gritsch, trans. Charles M. Jacobs and Eric W. Gritsch (Philadelphia: Fortress Press, 1966), 150.

[2] Herbert H. Farmer, *The Servant of the Word* (London: Nisbet and Co., 1941).

[3] Ibid., 86.

[4] All Scripture quotations in this chapter are from the New American Standard Version.

Chapter 2

■ ■ ■

THE FOOLISHNESS OF PREACHING

James Montgomery Boice

*J*once asked a number of people which verses came to mind when they thought about preaching. I had already gone to one of the concordances and looked up verses where the English words *preaching, preacher,* or *preach* occur, and I found that, even in these cases, which do not reflect all occurrences of the Greek and Hebrew root words (these are also translated "proclaim," "make known," "speak," and so on), there are 150 verses. But when I began to ask my question, people referred again and again to one verse, 1 Corinthians 1:21, which says, "God was pleased through the foolishness of what was preached to save those who believe."

I think that says something about the way many people regard what they hear coming from the pulpit. They think of it as foolishness. In the minds of many, the content of preaching, and perhaps even the delivery of the sermon itself, is a very foolish thing.

Is preaching really foolishness? It obviously is in some sense because Paul uses that word. Indeed, preachers will often say that there are times when they feel foolish as they try to bring a word from God to those living in the midst of a secular culture. Yet when we look at the passage from which that word comes, it is perfectly evident, even on a very superficial reading, that the apostle is using this word *foolishness* in a specialized sense. He is talking about that which is foolish in the world's eyes, but which in actuality is the wisdom of God unto salvation.

Paul makes this statement in a very interesting context. In this passage, he speaks not only of foolishness and wisdom, but also of weakness and power (a parallel contrast) and signs versus what we would probably call the foundation stone of revealed religion.

Paul was one of those rare individuals who moved quite easily among diverse cultures. He was a Jew, but he had grown up in a Roman town and was greatly influenced by Greek culture. So he moved equally well within Jewish, Greek, and Roman communities. Everywhere he went he preached Christ. He found that he did not have exactly the same problem when he moved among the Greeks as when he moved among the Romans, or when he moved among Romans as when he moved among the Jews. Each of these cultures had its own particular difficulty where the gospel was concerned.

The Romans' difficulty was that they were proud of their power. They ruled the world. Their legions held the barbarians at bay. Their naval power had brought order to the Mediterranean. Their soldiers kept the roads open and the brigands in their place. They controlled the greatest empire the world had ever seen. They were proud of their power. When the apostle spoke to the Romans in the context of the Roman culture, it was natural that the Jesus he preached (crucified under a Roman governor) seemed the epitome of weakness. As Paul spoke to the Romans, with their great concern for power, he had to show that, although Jesus is in a sense the weakness of God, this weakness of God was actually a power able to transform men and women. In Romans he says, "The gospel . . . is the power of God for the salvation of everyone who believes" (Rom. 1:16).[1]

With Jews the situation was not the same. If the Roman mentality was that of a military man who believes that the most important thing is strength, the Jewish mentality was what we might compare to the cults of our day. That is, the Jews wanted a sign; they wanted visible demonstrations. That is why they were always asking Jesus for miracles. They did not like the signs He gave because they did not like Him, just as people today do not like the words of the Bible because they do not like the Bible's God. They say, "If only God would say something; if only God would speak to me." But God has spoken. They do not accept it because they do not like Him.

In the same way, the Jews were asking for miracles. To Jews, Jesus was a stumbling block. But Paul maintained that far from being a stumbling block, the gospel of Christ was actually a foundation, a block over which one could stumble but which was actually the foundation stone of revealed religion.

This is the context in which Paul talks about foolishness. But in writing to the church at Corinth, he has a Greek mentality in mind. Greece had lost the power it once had under Philip of Macedon and Alexander the Great. That dominion was gone. But what the Greeks did have (and the Romans did not, at least not to the same degree) was wisdom. Greece produced the great philosophers. Greece provided the teachers. In most wealthy Roman homes, there was a slave who was responsible for the education of the children, and nine times out of ten he was a Greek. The Greeks were proud of this wisdom. When the early ambassadors of the gospel came, proclaiming that the ineffable God had become man in human flesh in order to die for our salvation, that contradicted everything the Greeks understood about philosophy. The basic principle of their philosophy was that mind was separated from matter, that spirit was separated from flesh. It was inconceivable to the Greek that there could be an incarnation. So what happened when Paul preached in Athens? They laughed, because his message seemed foolish. What Paul had to say to the Greeks was that this message, which appears to be foolishness, and which is communicated in a manner that is conceived to be the height of folly, is actually the wisdom of God.

On the basis of 1 Corinthians 1:21, we can say that preaching is that wise means of God by which the wisdom of the world is shown to be foolishness, and the folly of the gospel, as the world conceives it, is shown to be true wisdom.

Preaching Leads to Conversions

Why is preaching so important? It obviously is. If you look over the whole of the Bible and ask which of the characters in the Bible were preachers, you'll find that nearly all were. There were exceptions, of course. But you'll find that most of the Bible's male characters fall into this category. The New Testament looks back to Noah and calls him a "preacher of righteousness" (2 Peter 2:5). Enoch is declared to be a preacher. Martin Luther thought that all the antediluvians going right back to Adam were preachers. The prophets were preachers. So were many kings. The apostles and the apostles' disciples, people like Timothy, Titus, John Mark, Silas and others, were preachers. Preaching is obviously important in the biblical revelation. But the question is, "Why? Why is preaching so important as a means of grace?"

The obvious answer is that preaching is a means of conversion. It is by the preaching of the Word that God moves in the hearts and lives of people to turn them from sin to Jesus Christ. In Romans 10:14–15 Paul writes along these lines: "How, then, can they call on the one they have not believed in? And how can they believe in the one of whom they have not heard? And how can they hear without someone preaching to them? And how can they preach unless they are sent?"

This is one of the apostle Paul's great theological chains. The best-known of these chains occurs a few pages earlier in Romans: "Those God foreknew he also predestined to be conformed to the likeness of his Son. . . . Those he predestined, he also called; those he called, he also justified; those he justified, he also glorified" (Rom. 8:29–30). There you have an ascending chain beginning with the foreknowledge of God and proceeding through predestination, effectual calling, justification and glorification. That is the way Paul's mind operated.

Here in Romans 10, we find the same thing. But here he does not trace the chain forward, as it were—that is, from where we are now (or from the past) to where we are going to be in the future—but rather backward. He says: "Here are people who believe. Let's trace this back and see what the origins of that belief were." So he goes back from calling upon the name of Christ, to believing on the name of Christ, to hearing the name of Christ, to preaching, and the fact that preachers are sent out by God.

Calling upon Christ corresponds to that moment of personal commitment in which we speak to God in prayer, saying: "Yes, I understand these things and I do believe that Jesus died on the cross not just to be a Savior, but to be my Savior. Now I promise to follow him as my Savior and Lord." That is calling upon Christ.

But Paul says: "Even before that there is this matter of belief. No one calls on Christ until he or she first believes on Him." This concerns the content of the gospel. Faith is more than an intellectual assent to certain things. Faith has several elements. It has content or knowledge. It has the warming of the heart. It has a volitional element or commitment. All are important, but at the beginning is this matter of content. People have to know Him on whom they are to call, because no one can call on Christ for salvation who does not understand who He is and what He has done.

But how are they to understand? Paul answers, "They have to hear." How can they believe unless they hear about Christ?

Then he asks, "And how are they to hear?" Obviously, the way they are to hear is by preaching. Someone has to go and let this message of salvation, centered in the Lord Jesus Christ, be known to them. This is the way of conversion, because what God does in preaching is take His Word, which is not the mere word of men but the Word of God, and use it in a supernatural way to create spiritual life within the heart of the one listening.

I think the verse that is most helpful in explaining what happens in the matter of regeneration is 1 Peter 1:23. Peter is speaking there of how we are born again: "You have been born again, not of perishable seed, but of imperishable, through the living and enduring Word of God." When Peter says that we are born again of imperishable seed, I do not believe that he is talking about the kind of seed you plant in the ground. That image is used elsewhere. It is used especially of the resurrection: the seed is planted in the ground, it dies, it rises again. But in this text, Peter is using the word *seed* to mean the male element in human procreation. He is talking about new birth, and therefore illustrates this spiritual birth with physical birth. He says we are born again spiritually in a way that is analogous to how we are born in a physical sense.

What is necessary in order for a new life to come into being? You have to have the sperm of the father and the egg or ovum of the mother. They have to come together. Peter is saying that this is what happens in the new birth. God first of all plants the ovum of saving faith in the heart of the man or woman, because even faith is not from ourselves; it is the gift of God, not by works, so that no one can boast (Eph. 2:8–9). Then God takes His living Word, the seed of spiritual procreation, and allows that Word to be proclaimed in such a way that it goes into the person through the gate of the ears, through hearing, and penetrates the ovum of faith. As a result, there is a spiritual conception; there is new life.

This life begins to grow within, and just as in the case of pregnancy there is a period when a woman is not even aware that she is pregnant, so there can be the same thing spiritually. The life is there, but the person does not yet know what has happened. However, things are starting to change. The person is beginning to have an interest in spiritual things. He finds himself hungering for the Word of God. He reads it. He begins to feed upon it. Then, as the months go by (sometimes longer and sometimes shorter), there is the point in a service when someone may say, "If you want to receive Jesus as your Savior, put up your hand," and so he puts up his hand and comes forward and the counselor says, "Well, now you're born again." That is indeed how it may seem, but actually he was alive when the Word did its work. It is just that now the birth has taken place.

This is what makes preaching so exciting! The hardest day of the week for me is Sunday. It is also the best day of the week. The thing that makes it the best is that I never know what is going to happen. I come to church. I do not know who is going to be there. I preach. I do not know all the problems of the people I am preaching to. I know some of them, and I try to be as sensitive as I can, but one generally does not know the deep things in the heart. People sit and listen, each with his or her own problems, all at their own particular points along a line of spiritual pilgrimage. God takes the Word that is preached and speaks it to the heart, and afterward somebody will come up and say: "I don't know how you knew it, but what you said was exactly the thing I needed to hear. How did you know it? Did somebody tell you about me? Somebody must have." I also have had people get angry and say, "So-and-so told you about me and you were preaching at me." I did not even know who they were, but the Holy Spirit has a way of applying the Word forcefully. That is the way He brings about conversions.

One of my predecessors at Tenth Presbyterian Church, Donald Grey Barnhouse, used to say that when he preached to an audience, he used to think of them as barrels sitting on the pews. Most of them were empty. But some of them had gunpowder inside, and his job was to produce explosions. He did it by striking the matches of the Word and throwing them into the barrels. When he hit one that had gunpowder, there would be an explosion. God put the gunpowder there. Then, as the Word was preached, there was a spiritual ignition or rebirth. This is one of the reasons we should value preaching so highly.

Preaching Builds Believers and Local Churches

Preaching is important as a means of grace not merely because it is used of God to bring about conversions, but also because it is used for our sanctification, that is, our growth in holiness once we are born again. If you look back in your life and ask what God has most used in your life to make you grow, you will find that in the vast majority of cases it is preaching. I know that to be true in my own life. It is not that other elements were not present. I had the sacraments, Christian literature, others praying for me, and fellowship groups. But the thing God used most for my growth was the faithful exposition of the Word. That Word took hold of me so that years later, when I would hear something different, I could not believe it because I knew it was not true. The preaching of the Word that I had heard in my earlier days held me and led me as God continued the work He had begun so many years before.

Preaching is also the primary means of growth for the local church. There is a great deal of debate about this in our day, but it is the preaching of the Word that God most uses to build up a church, not only numerically but above all (and far more importantly) in the spiritual depth and understanding of the people who make up the congregation.

When we talk about the importance of preaching, preachers are inclined (modestly) to say, "Well, after all, no one is indispensable." And, of course, that is true, if we understand it in the right way. But it is false if we understand it in the wrong way. It is true that God does not need us. God does not need us to glorify Him. God does not need us to worship Him. God does not need us to proclaim the gospel. If the people at the time of Christ's entry into Jerusalem had failed to cry out, the stones would have done so, Jesus said. God is well able to raise up preachers from stones. But at the same time it is true that if God has called a man to be a preacher in a particular situation, that man is, by the calling and disposition of God, indispensable for that situation. If he gives good leadership and provides good teaching from the Word, that church will go forward. If he fails to do it, that church will not go forward.

Many things are talked about as necessary for the health and growth of the church today. People talk about certain programs as essential. It is true that they are important. We have such a diversified culture that people have their own individual problems. The family is fragmented, and the kind of reinforcement along Christian lines that ought to take place in homes does not always take place. The church is trying to minister specifically at these points through programs. Still, if you think back to the time of the Great Awakening in this country, you will realize that churches at that time had hardly any programs at all, at least nothing that we would recognize as programs. There were no youth groups, no graded Sunday schools, no bowling leagues, no baseball teams. But those churches were healthy. Why? Because they had the faithful preaching of the Word.

Do you know what is said to be the single most important factor for the growth of a church in California? The size of the parking lot! If your church has a big parking lot, it becomes a big church. So what a church must do, you see, is to get as much land as it can right off the bat.

But what is *essential*? It is the preaching and teaching of the Word of God, because as that is done God the Holy Spirit speaks through that Word to the hearts of Christian people (and unbelievers, too) and provides not only the numbers but the kind of leadership in character and commitment that is necessary if a church is to go forward. When that happens, we can change all sorts of things. The church may be deprived of a lot, but the body, which is the true church, is there and grows.

I do not think it is too much to say that preaching really is an essential means, perhaps even the most important means, of grace. If that is the case, then we should be very careful in our Christian lives to expose ourselves to the best teaching and attend the best churches available.

What Kind of Preachers?

What kind of preachers do we need? If you are choosing a church, you want to look for the right kind of preacher. If you are on a pulpit committee, you are responsible for knowing how to look.

First, we need preachers who are born again. It should not be necessary to say that; it seems self-evident. Yet it is necessary to say it because so many preachers are not born again. There are men standing in prominent pulpits of this land, thousands of pulpits, who are not regenerate.

Probably the second most influential sermon that has ever been preached on the North American continent was on this theme. The most important and most significant sermon very likely was Jonathan Edwards' "Sinners in the Hands of an Angry God." Number two was preached in 1740, one year earlier than Edwards' sermon, and was titled "The Dangers of an Unconverted Ministry." The preacher was Gilbert Tennent. He said: "Look into the congregations of unconverted ministers and see what a sad security reigns there, not a soul convinced [that is, converted] that can be heard of for many years together, and yet the ministers are easy because they say they do their duty. These caterpillars labor to devour every green thing and the chief object is not to preach the new birth but to keep the people in their inter-est." Then he said, "Natural men [that is, unconverted men] have no call of God to the ministerial work. So if a godly man finds himself in a church or denomination in which such natural men hold rule, then it is both lawful and expedient to go from there to hear godly persons."

You can imagine that Tennent's words made many preachers angry. But he told the truth, not only for his day but for ours. It is a sad thing that many preachers in our day are unconverted. Conversion is the first essential of true preaching.

Second, those who would be the kind of preacher God uses, whose preaching is a means of grace, must believe the Bible. The Bible is where God speaks, and it is the preacher's primary task—not his whole task, but his primary task—to exposit that Word.

I have had occasion to speak on this subject in many places, and I find that as I share some of my experiences and the things I have heard, lay audiences in particular are astounded to be told that so many ministers really do not believe the Bible. Yet that is the case. Ministers are somewhat reluctant to say what they really believe because, if they do, their congregations are likely to get rid of them. They will be out looking for another job. But they do say what they believe in the company of other ministers.

I was speaking at a gathering of leaders in a mainline denomination a number of years ago. When I got to the end of my paper, there was a question-and-answer period, and a professor at one of the theological seminaries stood up. He disagreed with everything I had said, and he took a long time to do it.

At one point, because I had mentioned the historical Jesus, he said: "There is no such thing as the historical Jesus. Don't you know that every one of the gospels was written to contradict the other gospels?" (I didn't know that! I thought they were different portraits of the same Christ, that they were complementary.) At another point in my remarks, I had said that Jesus was going to come again. This professor replied, "We have got to get it into our heads that Jesus is never coming back and all things are going to continue as they have from the beginning." Now, that did not surprise me, because Peter said: "In the last days scoffers will come. . . . They will say, 'Where is this coming He promised? For since our fathers died, everything goes on as it has since the beginning of creation'" (2 Peter 3:3–4). That man was quoting Peter verbatim, though I do not think he knew what he was doing! It was probably the residue of his evangelical upbringing, which he had rebelled against. But there he was, teaching unbelief to the students in our seminaries.

I have a friend who has worked for renewal in that same denomination. On one occasion, after he had been arguing a point, a liberal minister came up to him and said: "Why are you always quoting the Bible when you stand up to argue a point? Don't you know that nobody believes the Bible anymore?"

Some years ago, a news report crossed my desk regarding a three-day national seminar of the Southern Baptist Christian Life Commission. One of the speakers was Robert Bratcher, a main translator of the *Good News for Modern Man* Bible. He said:

> Only willful ignorance or intellectual dishonesty can account for the claim that the Bible is inerrant and infallible . . . . No truth-loving, God-respecting, Christ-honoring believer should be guilty of such heresy. To invest the Bible with the qualities of inerrancy and infallibility is to idolatrize it, to transform it into a false God . . . . Often in the past and still too often in the present to affirm that the Bible is the Word of God implies that the words of the Bible are the words of God. [Yes, I thought that is what we were affirming—almost always in the past and not nearly enough in the present.] Such simplistic and absolute terms divest the Bible altogether of its humanity and remove it from the relativism of the historical process. No one seriously claims that all the words of the Bible are the very words of God. [That, at least, is wrong, because I seriously claim it.] . . .
>
> Quoting what the Bible says in the context of its history and culture is not necessarily relevant or helpful, and may be a hindrance in trying to meet and solve the problems we face. . . . Even words spoken by Jesus in Aramaic in the thirties of the first century and preserved in writing in Greek 35 to 50 years later, do not necessarily wield compelling or authoritative authority over us . . . It is the height of presumption and arrogance to say, "I know this is God's will, and I am doing it."[2]

That is what we are up against, and it is a sad state of affairs. It is not unnecessary to say that the men who stand in the pulpits must be born again and must believe the Bible.

Third, not only must we who preach believe the Bible, we must obey the Bible. Those of us who make a point of affirming the Bible's authority must take note of this especially, because it is very easy to make a crusade of something while not actually allowing it to influence your life. You can wave a banner. You can say, "Oh, yes, I believe in the Bible." You can get people to cheer. But then you can go out and do something that you know is perfectly contrary to what the Bible says. You can even know the Bible well enough to quote it back to God and yet disobey it.

Jonah was a preacher whom God told to go to Nineveh, but he would not do it. He ran away. Indeed, he was going to Tarshish until God intercepted him and brought him back. God took His election of Jonah to that particular ministry so seriously that in God's sight Jonah was absolutely indispensable. So He brought him back and used him to effect one of the greatest revivals the world has ever seen.

However, at the end of the story Jonah was unhappy, and he explained why he did not obey when God sent him to Nineveh. Why was it? Was it the danger? Well, Nineveh was a dangerous place. The Ninevites were not nice people. When they did not like somebody, they cut off his head. If there were a lot of people they did not like, they cut off all their heads and piled them up in a great pyramid in the city square. It was their idea of a visual aid to learning. Jonah might have said: "I don't want my head on that pile. It's too dangerous. I won't go." Yet there is not a word in the Bible to indicate that this is why he refused.

Was it the difficulty? He might have said: "Me? Jonah? One man? A Jew? How can I possibly influence all those mighty people? I can't do it; I'm just a nobody. I have to stay home." There is not a word to indicate that this was the reason, either.

What was it? At the end of the book, Jonah says, in effect: "The reason I'm unhappy is that You, O God, caused a revival among the enemies of my people and so spared them. The reason why I wouldn't go to Nineveh in the first place is that I knew that was what You were going to do. You were sending me to preach a message of judgment, to say, 'If you don't repent in forty days, you're going to go to hell.' But You didn't need me to go and tell them they were going to go to hell; they'd have gone to hell just as quickly without my preaching. You were sending me with a message of judgment so they would repent. And do You want to know how I knew that? I read it in Your book. I read it right there in the thirty-second chapter of Exodus, where it says, 'The LORD, the LORD, the compassionate and gracious God, slow to anger, abounding in love and faithfulness, maintaining love to thousands, and forgiving wickedness, rebellion, and sin. Yet he does not leave the guilty unpunished; he punishes the children and their children for the sin of the fathers to the third and fourth generation'" (Ex. 34:6–7; cf. Jonah 4:2). Do you see the problem? It was not a question of Jonah's not knowing the Word or not believing the Word. It was a question of obedience.

God's Enoch

We need preachers who will walk with God. That is, we need preachers who will walk with God in a regular, steady, at times unspectacular and often difficult way, week by week, month by month, year by year, because this work is not always a spectacular business.

A great illustration of this is the walk of the first explicit preacher in the Bible. I told you Luther's opinion of the antediluvians—he talked about all of them being preachers in their times, and certainly priests in their own homes. But most of them are not explicitly said to be preachers. One man is: Enoch. He is mentioned in the fifth chapter of Genesis, where we are told twice that he "walked with God," and that is why I refer to him.

It is an interesting feature of this man that we are told more about him in the New Testament than in the Old. There are four verses about him in the Old Testament as opposed to three in the New, but there are more words in the New than in the Old (ninety words in the New Testament compared to about fifty in the Old). Jude contains some teaching about him (vv. 14–15), and his name is mentioned in Hebrews 11:5.

Jude identifies Enoch as the "seventh from Adam." Can you think of anybody else in the Bible who is identified as the seventh from anybody, or even the fifth or the fourth? I cannot, except in the genealogy of Christ, where there are fourteen generations from segment to segment. Why does Jude refer to Enoch as the seventh from Adam? The reason emerges when we examine that fifth chapter of Genesis in light of the fourth, because in Genesis 4 and 5 we find not one but two Enochs. Genesis 4 gives the line of Cain, the ungodly line. Genesis 5 gives the line of Seth, the godly line. And there is an Enoch in the line of Seth as well as in the line of Cain. Enoch in the line of Cain is the third from Adam, that is, Cain's son. Enoch in the line of Seth is the seventh from Adam. He was the son of Jared, and his son was Methuselah. Jude is saying: "I want to hold up a great example of godly living: Enoch. But I don't want you to make a mistake. I don't want you to imitate the wrong one. God had His Enoch. The Devil also had his Enoch. I want you to imitate God's Enoch."

This gives a great principle for understanding much of life. The Devil has his people; God has His people. The Devil has his doctors; God has His doctors. The Devil has his housewives; God has His housewives. The Devil has his lawyers; God has His lawyers. Here in Jude, God is saying, "The Devil has his preachers and I have My preachers. Imitate My men."

Jude also tells us something about Enoch's preaching. He says that Enoch had a message of judgment. As I read Genesis, I think this was new. I think these early believers lived in hope of the coming of the Deliverer, but they did not understand much about His coming. The first messianic prophecy, called the *protoevangelium*, occurs in Genesis 3 in the context of the curse upon the serpent. God said: "I'm sending a deliverer. He'll be the seed of the woman. He'll crush Satan's head, though Satan will bruise His heel" (cf. Gen. 3:15). In those early days, this was the hope for which Adam and Eve and the others lived. But along came Enoch, who had received this revelation: "God is indeed coming, but before He comes as deliverer He is going to come as Judge. There is going to be a flood." His message was, "See, the Lord is coming with thousands upon thousands of His holy ones to judge everyone" (Jude 14b–15a).

But why was God coming to judge everyone? Because of our wickedness, Enoch said. He is coming "to convict all the ungodly of all the ungodly acts they have done in the ungodly way, and of all the harsh words ungodly sinners have spoken against Him" (15b). How many times does Enoch say "ungodly" in that passage? Four times! There are only twenty-eight words in that segment of this passage in my Bible, but four of them are the word *ungodly*. One-seventh of all Enoch's recorded preaching focused on the ungodliness of his age.

What is the point? Simply that these concerns go together with what is said about Enoch back in Genesis, where it says, "Enoch walked with God." Jude used the word *ungodly* four times, but in Genesis it says twice, "Enoch walked with

God." When Enoch had lived sixty-five years, he became the father of Methuselah. And after he became the father of Methuselah, Enoch walked with God three hundred years and had other sons and daughters. Altogether Enoch lived 365 years. He began to walk with God in a special way when he was 65 years old. I think that is when he got his revelation of coming judgment. He knew what was coming. He saw the ungodliness of his age. He had believed in God before, but now he was determined to walk with God in the midst of this ungodliness. He walked with God and he walked with God and he walked with God, and when God took him at age 365, Genesis says of him, "Enoch walked with God."

That was no casual stroll. Three hundred years is a long time. What kept Enoch walking with God for three hundred years? He had an awareness of judgment coming. He had a sensitivity to the ungodliness of the age. And he drew closer to God as the reality of these things pressed in upon him. The way to graph it would be to make a circle, space these three items around the circle, and then show by arrows that each one influenced the other. The more Enoch was aware of the judgment, the more sensitive he was to sin. The more sensitive he was to sin, the closer he wanted to walk with God. The closer he walked with God, the more clearly he saw that judgment was necessary. Or the other way: the more clearly he saw the judgment coming, the closer he wanted to walk with God, and the closer he walked with God the more sensitive he was to ungodliness.

If you keep close to God, you will keep from sin. But if you sin persistently, you will fall away from God. Then you will rename the sin. You will not talk about pride, the great sin; you will call it "self-esteem," "self-worth," or what is "due to me." You will not talk about gluttony and materialism; you will talk about "the good life." You will not talk about disobedience; you will talk about "shortcomings." You will not talk about the Ten Commandments and your violation of them; you will talk about your "mistakes." It is only when you draw close to God that these things will become increasingly sinful in your sight. Only then will they work together to make you a preacher committed to calling men and women to repentance and faith in Christ before the judgment comes.

I mentioned three texts in the Bible that speak about Enoch: Genesis 5:21–24; Jude 14–15, and Hebrews 11:5. I close with this last text because of something that is said there about Enoch: "By faith Enoch was taken from this life, so that he did not experience death; he could not be found, because God had taken him away. For before he was taken, he was commended as one who pleased God."

We are all anxious to please. One reason why we have such a dearth of leadership in our age is that those who could and should be leaders are so anxious to please people, their constituency or their superiors, that they are afraid to lead and so become paralyzed. We all have this desire. We are pleased when people are pleased. When I preach a sermon that I am pleased with and I go to the door and somebody says, "Oh, I really did enjoy that sermon," I am pleased. But if it comes right down to a choice between pleasing men and pleasing God, there is no choice for the one who claims to be a servant of the Most High. We must please God!

We must so live, act, preach, and testify that at the day of final reckoning, when we stand before the One who made us and called us into service, it will not be said of us, "Here is one who sought all through life to please others," but rather, "Here is one who above all else determined to please God." When you seek a minister for your congregation, look for that. Look for someone who is determined to please God. You will be blessed. Your ministers will be blessed. And the day will come when the Lord Himself will say to you and to them: "Welcome into My presence, you good and faithful servant. Enter into the joy of your Lord."

Endnotes

[1] All Scripture quotations in this chapter are from the New International Version.

[2] Robert Bratcher, quoted in *The Baptist Courier*, April 2, 1981.

Chapter 3

■ ■ ■

EXPOSITORY PREACHING

Derek W. H. Thomas

*A*ccording to the legendary golfer Jack Nicklaus, the best thing he ever did was to discover the "fundamentalist" teacher Jack Grout, who taught him the basics that he has followed ever since. Great preachers, like great golfers, follow basic rules. The more they practice these rules, the better they become.

One such rule, put succinctly in English prose that now sounds dated, but which is as needful now as when it was first penned, comes from the Directory for the Publick Worship of God, written in 1645 by the Westminster Assembly of Divines. When raising a point from the text, the directory says, preachers are to ensure that "it be a truth contained in or grounded on that text, that the hearers may discern how God teacheth it from thence."[1] In other words, preaching must enable those who hear it to understand their Bibles.

In laying down this principle, the divines were following the first book on homiletics to be produced by the English Reformation, William Perkins' *The Arte of Prophecying* (1617), which included this instruction: "The Word of God alone is to be preached, in its perfection and inner consistency. Scripture is the exclusive subject of preaching, the only field in which the preacher is to labour."[2]

As incredible as it seems, Perkins found it necessary to underline the fact that preachers are to preach the Bible and the Bible *alone*. As Paul urged Timothy, the preacher's task is to "preach the word" (2 Tim. 4:2).[3]

Earlier, Paul had assured the Corinthians that he and his companions were not "like so many, peddlers of God's Word" (2 Cor. 2:17). The word Paul employs here, *kapeleuô*, is rendered variously as "peddle," "corrupt," or "deal deceitfully"; the New Living Translation renders the verse, "we are not like those hucksters—and there are many of them—who preach just to make money." This word comes from the world of ancient tavern-keeping. It suggests the practice of "blending, adulterating, and giving bad measure."[4] Paul was concerned for purity and honesty in handling the Scriptures.

He charged young Timothy again to present himself to God "as one approved, a worker who has no need to be ashamed, rightly handling the word of truth" (2 Tim. 2:15). The word that is translated in many versions as "to handle" or "to divide" actually means "to cut" (*orthotomeo*).[5] Timothy was to drive a straight path through the Word of God and not deviate to the left or to the right. He was to "preach the word," meaning not only that he was to preach from the Bible, but that he was to *expound* the particular passage he was preaching on because Scripture, as Paul reminds Timothy, is "breathed out by God" (2 Tim. 3:16).

Expository preaching is a *necessary* corollary of the doctrine of the God-breathed nature of Scripture. The idea is not so much that God breathed *into* the Scriptures, but that the Scriptures are the product of His breathing *out*. Independent of what we may feel about the Bible as we read it, Scripture maintains a "breath of God" quality. Thus, the preacher is to make God's Word known and make it understandable. He is to limit himself to it without adding or subtracting. As Alec Motyer has written: "An expository ministry is the proper response to a God-breathed Scripture. . . . Central to it all is that concern which the word 'exposition' itself enshrines: a display of what is there."[6]

Such word-focused ministry, based on divinely given Scripture (as Paul makes plain to the church at Ephesus), fulfills four goals all at once: it builds up the church in faith and knowledge; it brings believers to maturity marked by spiritual stability; it produces a people whose lives are full of integrity; and it equips the church for service so that each member is engaged in ministry to others (Eph. 4:12–16).

From Calvin to Boice

Belief in the divine origin of Scripture led John Calvin in the sixteenth century to a commitment to expository/exegetical preaching. Commenting on 2 Timothy 3:16–17, the *locus classicus* of biblical inspiration, the Genevan Reformer insisted,

"We owe to the Scriptures the same reverence as we owe to God, since it has its only source in Him and has nothing of human origin mixed with it."[7]

Therefore, the preaching of Scripture requires the most thorough preparation. At the same time that Calvin preached through 1 and 2 Timothy on Sundays, he was preaching on Job and then Deuteronomy on weekdays. Commenting on Deuteronomy 6:16, Calvin writes:

> If I should step up into the pulpit, without vouchsafing to look upon any book, and fondly imagine to say thus in my self, "Truth, when I come thither, God will give me enough whereof to speak," and in the meanwhile I hold scorn to read, or to study aforehand what I shall speak, and come hither without minding how to apply the Holy Scripture to the edification of the people, by reason whereof I should play the presumptuous fool, and God would put me to shame for mine overboldness.[8]

Though Calvin is fond of the word *dictation* when he refers to the inspiration of Scripture,[9] that does not mean Calvin saw no place for, or implications derived from, the *humanness* of Scripture. Early in his *Institutes of the Christian Religion*, he comments on the "elegant" and "brilliant" style of some of the prophets, the "sweet" and "pleasing" styles of David and Isaiah, and the "harsher" styles of Amos, Jeremiah, and Zechariah.[10] Thus, Calvin gave due diligence to the meaning of the words of Scripture, to grammar and syntax, to literary genre, to authorial intent, to context, and to a hermeneutic of harmony that a belief in inspiration requires. But at the end of the day, Calvin could say in his last will and testament, "I have endeavored, both in my sermons and also in my writings and commentaries, to preach the Word purely and chastely, and faithfully to interpret His sacred Scriptures."[11]

During the years 1549–1560, Calvin employed Denis Ragunier to record word for word every sermon he preached. More than two thousand of his sermons exist today for us to examine for our profit, and their consistency of style continues to amaze. Though Calvin never wrote a formal manual on homiletics, his sermons disclose a commitment to the discipline of expository preaching and the *lectio continua* ("continuous expositions") method.

As for the latter, it is not essential to do what Calvin did (or the "golden-mouthed" John Chrysostom before him[12]), that is, to preach consecutively through the books of the Bible (in Calvin's case) six to ten verses at a time. Textual sermons can and should be equally expository, that is, committed to the discipline of sound exegetical principles. But history reveals that the benefits of the *lectio continua* method of preaching are considerable and essential in eras of biblical illiteracy. Nothing could illustrate Calvin's commitment to it better than the fact that following his enforced exile in Strasbourg (having been evicted from Geneva on Easter Sunday 1538), Calvin returned in September 1541 to pick up precisely where he had left off three and half years before.[13]

In our own recent history, few have raised the importance of expository preaching within the discipline of homiletics more than Bryan Chapell, John MacArthur, D. Martyn Lloyd-Jones, and James Montgomery Boice. Each one has contributed to the conviction of the value and *necessity* of expository preaching.

Chapell has done more than most to recover a zeal for expository preaching amongst his own constituents and beyond. His *Christ-Centered Preaching: Redeeming the Expository Sermon* is justly applauded quite simply as one of the best single-volume works on preaching to emerge in a century.[14] In it, he defines an expository sermon as that which "requires that it expound Scripture by deriving from a specific text main points and subpoints that disclose the thought of the author, cover the scope of the passage, and are applied to the lives of the listeners."[15]

Some have commented that much expository preaching is so bad that it calls into question the method. It cannot be denied that bad expository preaching exists. Much of it is in the form of a running commentary, with little attention to structure and form. As one who now teaches homiletics at a seminary, I find myself needing to distinguish a sermon from something that sounds like the fruits of culling several commentaries (even if they are *good* ones). The necessary discipline of understanding the text is only the first step in constructing a sermon. There is more to preaching than imparting information, as Chapell insists. Unless sermons address the affections, they have failed as sermons. In the deceptively simple advice of the Cambridge preacher, Charles Simeon (1759–1836), "The understanding must be informed, but in a manner, however, which *affects the heart*, either to comfort the hearers, or to excite them to acts of piety, repentance, or holiness."[16]

MacArthur writes in *Rediscovering Expository Preaching*, "The only logical response to inerrant Scripture . . . is to preach it *expositionally*."[17] Defining *exegesis* as "the skillful application of sound hermeneutical principles to the biblical text of the original language with a view to understanding and declaring the author's intended meaning both to the immediate and subsequent audiences,"[18] MacArthur insists that the church's loss of commitment to expository preaching is due to what he calls "the legacy of liberalism." Robbed of any confidence in the Scriptures themselves through textual or source criticism, preachers lost sight of the goal: making the Scriptures known. Instead of explaining the Scriptures, preachers felt the need to apologize for much of its content and supply their own rhetorical skills to make up for its perceived deficiencies. MacArthur is right: only in the context of a firm belief in Scripture's inerrancy has expository preaching thrived.

Lloyd-Jones's lectures at Westminster Seminary (Philadelphia) in the spring of 1969 resulted in what has proved to be a classic work on preaching in the twentieth century, *Preaching and Preachers*.[19] In one sense, it is much more than a work on the *mechanics* of preaching, for it covers a wide variety of issues. It contains the reflections of a great preacher eager to inculcate much more than *how* to construct a sermon. Early in the book, Lloyd-Jones issues a warning about abusing Scripture by making it fit a particular system of truth. This warning betrays his concern for proper execution of exegetical disciplines in preaching:

> It is wrong for a man to impose his system violently on any particular text; but at the same time it is vital that his interpretation of any particular text should be checked and controlled by this system, this body of doctrine and of truth which is found in the Bible. The tendency of some men who have a systematic theology, which they hold very rigidly, is to impose this wrongly upon particular texts and so do violence to those texts. In other words they do not actually derive that particular doctrine from the text with which they are dealing at that point. The doctrine may be true but it does not arise from that particular text; and we must always be textual. That is what I meant by not 'imposing' your system upon a particular text or statement. The right use of systematic theology is, that when you discover a particular doctrine in your text you check it, and control it, by making sure that it fits into the whole body of biblical doctrine which is vital and essential.[20]

Boice believed in expository preaching and said so often. His four-volume set of sermons on Romans is rightly called *An Expositional Commentary*,[21] as is his five-volume set of sermons on John's Gospel[22] and similar works on Genesis,[23] the Psalms,[24] the Minor Prophets,[25] Acts,[26] Ephesians,[27] and Philippians.[28] These books were sermons before they ever saw the printed format. They are classic in style: simple, structured, highlighting main themes, alluding to other passages only to illustrate what is already drawn out of the text in question, and always applicatory. Few congregations in the twentieth century enjoyed such rich fare as did Tenth Presbyterian Church in Philadelphia during Boice's tenure as senor minister.

Bad Homiletical Models

Despite these books on preaching, bad homiletical models of expository preaching still exist. They come from various sources and are influenced by a variety of factors. Often it is not the model itself that is at fault, but the use made of it. They include:

1. *The Puritans.* With the exception of John Calvin, few men have influenced my thinking more than John Owen. To Owen I owe an understanding of sanctification and biblical spirituality that has preserved my sanity on more than one occasion. Owen's works are deservedly reprinted and studied. If banished to a desert island with the Bible and six books, I would bend every rule to ensure that all sixteen volumes of Owen's works were included as *one* book, and if that could not be done, then I would have to ensure that Volume 2, *On Communion with God,* was one of the six![29] To a man, the Puritans were committed to the *plain* preaching of the Word of God. Few have matched the expositional skills of Owen, Joseph Hall, Thomas Goodwin, Richard Sibbes, Richard Baxter, Thomas Manton, Stephen Charnock, or John Bunyan. On exegetical grounds, they stand shoulder to shoulder with the Denneys, Lightfoots, and Murrays of later centuries. The church would be greatly impoverished without Manton on James, Greenhill on Ezekiel, or Jenkyn on Jude. Their insights and contributions continue to profit the church.

Nevertheless, in the matter of *consecutive* expository preaching, the Puritans are not always a model for us to follow. To take an extreme example, we can safely say that Joseph Caryl, who took twenty-four years to expound the book of Job in 424 sermons (averaging ten sermons per chapter), was not a good model for preaching the book of Job or for expository preaching in general.[30] The Puritans show an admirable care in teasing out doctrine and even greater skill in application to those in diverse trials (which makes them invaluable reading to this day), but it is doubtful that there are any circumstances, then or now, that would justify such a prolonged series of sermons on one book. Speaking generally is always dangerous, but it is probably true to say that few young preachers can sustain a lengthy (and slow) series of expositions on a particular book of the Bible. Times have changed, as have our congregations, and it is wiser in most circumstances to move at a more rapid pace through the Scriptures than the Puritans did.

2. *D. Martyn Lloyd-Jones.* Possibly the greatest expositor/preacher of the twentieth century, Lloyd-Jones has had a considerable influence on the preaching styles of several generations of preachers on both sides of the Atlantic. In Britain especially, following the publication of Lloyd-Jones' expositions of Romans (sermons preached during a fourteen-year period, 1955–1968), many Reformed preachers attempted to follow Lloyd-Jones' preaching model.[31] The problem was that few, if any, could come close to the exegetical and homiletical skills of "the Doctor." Many a congregation was wearied by an overly ambitious series in the consecutive expository method, and by practitioners that weren't up to the task. What may be possible and desirable in one context may not be so in another due to several factors, including the giftedness and maturity of the preacher and the makeup of the congregation.[32] Some preachers have been drained by an overly-ambitious series that was beyond their giftedness to deliver. As a result, they have wisely retreated to safer shores.

3. *C. H. Spurgeon.* The Anglican Bishop J. C. Ryle, in a wonderful lecture called "Simplicity in Preaching," given at St. Paul's Cathedral, said of Spurgeon's preaching:

> I am not a bit ashamed to say that I often read the sermons of Mr. Spurgeon. I like to gather hints about preaching from all quarters. . . . Now when you read Mr. Spurgeon's sermons, note how clearly and perspicuously he divides a sermon, and fills each division with beautiful and simple ideas. How easily you grasp the meaning! . . . great truths, that hang to you like hooks of steel, and which . . . you never forget![33]

My acquaintance with and love for Spurgeon began in 1977, when a somewhat disillusioned friend offered me the complete set (sixty-two volumes) of his sermons, which he had just purchased and had found wanting! I have used them over and over ever since, sometimes with great delight and admiration, and sometimes (it has to be said) with dismay at his handling of the text.[34] Spurgeon's invariable style was textual, often focusing on one or two verses.[35] His *intent* was always to be expository; in *practice*, he could sometimes introduce matters into the sermon that did not properly emerge from the text, and he never engaged in consecutive expository preaching. Nevertheless, the salutary influence of the greatest Baptist preacher of the nineteenth century has been incalculable.

4. Redemptive-historical preaching. Those who favor what is called redemptive-historical preaching tend to be deeply critical of expository preaching styles of the past. They regard the homiletical styles of Augustine and Calvin as guilty of mixing Judeo-Christian theology with classical pagan methodology in their use of the grammatico-historical hermeneutic. Within the redemptive-historical model, there is a commitment to preaching the text and even doing so consecutively; as such, it *sounds* like expository preaching. But there is a (valid) concern to emphasize context within the overall structure of God's redemptive plan as it unfolds historically. Sermons of this sort spend a great deal of time detailing the flow of redemptive history, which, on first hearing, can be breathtaking if done well. But what often results from this hermeneutic is a certain predictability (a rehearsal of the history of redemption) that those who repeatedly hear it regard as "boring" and "irrelevant."

Indeed, in its fear of moralistic exegesis (*biographical* preaching is particularly criticized), application is noticeably absent from these sermons. There is much appeal to the mind, but little if any to the heart. Indeed, many sermons in this school of thought have no discernible application whatsoever, apart from the informative, that shapes the way we think. Some of the remarks in an otherwise masterly treatment of preaching by Sidney Greidanus fall under this criticism.[36]

These and other considerations have led some to abandon consecutive expository preaching altogether in favor of textual preaching. Such preaching, as we have seen, can be decidedly exegetical in nature. The sermon sticks to the text and seeks to expound the passage (or verse) according to the rules of sound interpretation. It is a method that has much to commend it, not least in that each Lord's Day brings forth "something new" that frees the preacher from the charge of predictability and sameness.

When the Eye Is Not on the Text

There are a variety of sermon types that fail to "display what is there." These include:

1. *The "I want to tell you what is on my heart" sermon.* It may begin with the text, but the text functions as a mere peg on which to hang the preacher's "concerns." Its hermeneutic is inadequate. It fails to look at the intention of God in the passage. What emerges is often full of passion but devoid of precision, earnest but effervescent, relevant but *un*-related.

2. *The "I have been reading Louis Berkhof's* Systematic Theology*" sermon.*[37] Instead of asking the question, "What is the intention of God?" it asks, "Where does this passage fit in my systematic theology?" or "What doctrine does this passage teach?" Both Reformed and dispensational schools fall into this practice regularly. They have a certain shape of truth, and this shape is going to be stretched and made to fit. Thus, sermons become defensive. These sermons are often better when dealing with Pauline epistles but go hopelessly astray when dealing in the genres of poetry or history. The sermons are often careful—too careful—in avoiding the barriers established by systematic theology, but fail to come right up close to them, as many texts of Scripture force us to do. In order to make the passage fit, it must be bent out of shape, and the result looks very different from what a cursory reading of the passage would suggest.[38]

3. *The "I have a seminary education and I am determined to let you know that" sermon.* In its extreme form, this kind of sermon becomes a lecture on the original meaning of the Greek or Hebrew. What belongs in the preacher's study is brought into the pulpit. There is enormous emphasis on the word study, syntax, Greek and/or Hebrew, archeology, textual variants, original intent, and cultural background. The vast research has as its aim a proper exegesis of the passage. But it fails to "bridge the gap between two horizons" (to borrow the language of Gadamer and Thiselton, and popularized by John Stott)[39] stretching from the world of the Bible to the world of the listener. The sermon sounds like a lecture because it *is* a lecture. It titillates the intellect, but fails to minister to the affections. Its delivery even (perhaps unintentionally) suggests that only the few—those endowed by special wisdom and insight—can possibly be trusted to understand what the Bible says. The sermon fails to underline the Reformational emphasis on the perspicuity of

Scripture: "that not only the learned, but the unlearned, in a due use of the ordinary means, may attain a sufficient understanding of [the Bible]."[40] A Reformed sacerdotalism has emerged, with the preacher squarely resident between the Bible and the listener.

4. *The "I am in such a hurry to apply this that you must forgive me for not showing you where I get this from" sermon.* The necessary study may well have been done, but the listener is unable to "discern how God teacheth it from thence." Listeners gain the impression that they are being lectured, that some hidden (and maybe not so hidden) agenda is at work. They do not come away having understood the passage better or with the impression that they could have discerned this for themselves.

The *Lectio Continua* Method

While it is, of course, possible (and sometimes desirable) to preach expository sermons *textually*—in Romans this week, in the Psalms the next, and in Haggai the following week—there is something about the very discipline of exposition that makes it impossible not to pick up the threads of an argument that begins in one chapter and runs on for several more. Few passages are complete in themselves, requiring little, if any, reference to preceding verses or what follows (individual psalms taken as *whole psalms* are one example, though not if only one or two verses of a particular psalm constitute the text). It is very difficult to read Paul without following a lengthy argument that unfolds over lengthy passages requiring a *series* of sermons to unpack. It might be helpful, then, to ask, "What are some of the advantages of the *consecutive* expository sermon?"[41] I'll conclude this chapter by summarizing what I see as six advantages of this methodology:

1. *Expository preaching introduces the congregation to the entire Bible.* J. W. Alexander writes, "All the more cardinal books of Scripture should be fully expounded in every church, if not once during the life of a single preacher, certainly during each generation; in order that no man should grow up without opportunity of hearing the great body of scriptural truth laid open."[42]

In an age of relative biblical illiteracy in many parts of the world, the need to preach the whole Bible, rather than serendipitously picking a text from here and there, is all the more urgent. Writing over a century ago, William Taylor opined,

I have seen a slimly attended second service gather back into itself all the half-day hearers that had absented themselves from it, and draw in others besides, through the adoption by the minister of just such a method as this; while the effect, even upon those who have dropped casually in upon a single discourse, has been to send them away with what one of themselves called "a new appetite for the Word of God."[43]

2. *Expository preaching* ensures that infrequently traveled areas of the Bible are covered. The inspired quality of Scripture (2 Tim. 3:16–17) implies that the whole canon—"all Scripture"—bears the mark of divine authorship. Our knowledge and holiness are hampered to the degree we neglect certain portions of Scripture. What preacher will preach from Zechariah, Jeremiah, or Revelation (except it be a favorite text or two) unless driven to it by a programmatic attempt to preach through the whole Bible? Large tracts of the Bible will never be touched unless the discipline of consecutive expository preaching forces the preacher to do so.

3. *Expository preaching prevents preachers from unwittingly shaping the way their hearers read their Bibles.* Large areas of the Bible are rarely read by many Christians. They arouse greater dread than the Mines of Moria did for Gandalf and Aragorn in *The Fellowship of the Ring*.[44] Consequently, the Bible is reduced to favorite verses, underlined or highlighted to provide steppingstones through murky waters. Preachers who jump from text to text, ignoring difficult sections of the Bible, reinforce this tendency. By contrast, consecutive expository preaching can inculcate sound habits of personal Bible study. The congregation can absorb the necessary principles of sound interpretation, almost by osmosis, through such repeated forays into relatively obscure passages from week to week in the pulpit.

When Paul asked the church at Colossae to pray that he might be able to preach "plainly" (Greek, *phanerosis*, unveiling, exposition), he was asking that he might bring out from the text what was inherently there. Paul, likewise, made the claim with respect to his preaching at Corinth that "by the open statement of the truth" he refused "to tamper with God's word" (2 Cor. 4:2). By renouncing distortion (tampering), the apostle insists that what he did was to "expose" (Greek, *phanerosis*) what was already there in the Word. Hearing that done, week after week, cannot but cement form and content.

One of the most heart-enriching experiences for any preacher is to hear someone bring something out of a text that reflects (albeit unwittingly) what he has
done countless times in the pulpit.[45] As Robert Dabney puts it:

> A prime object of pastoral teaching is to teach the people how to read the
> Bible for themselves. A sealed book cannot be interesting. If it be read without
> the key of comprehension, it cannot be instructive. Now, it is the preacher's
> business, in his public discourses, to give his people teaching by example, in
> the art of interpreting the Word: he should exhibit before them, in actual use,
> the methods by which the legitimate meaning is to be evolved. Fragmentary
> preaching, however brilliant, will never do this.[46]

Stott, in an interview given in 1995, speaks to this issue:

> We want to let the congregation into the secret as to how we have reached the
> conclusions we have reached as to what the Bible is actually saying. . . . And
> gradually, as you are doing this in the pulpit, the congregation is schooled not
> only in what the Bible teaches but in how we come to the congregation as to
> what it teaches. So we have to show the congregation what our hermeneutical
> methods are.[47]

4. Expository preaching is the only preaching method that exposes a congregation to the full range of Scripture's interests and concerns.[48] Why would a
preacher desire to choose as his subject divorce, polygamy, or incest other than
the fact that they arise naturally in the course of exposition?[49] Many a hearer will
accuse preachers of a conspiracy whenever the Word begins to "meddle" (as they
say in Mississippi). Happy is the preacher who can point to the text and say, "That
subject just happens to be in the passage we're studying this morning!" It is only
by the sustained use of the *lectio continua* method that large sections of Scripture
can be covered, including those areas less well known and traversed but containing
truth designed to shape us into Christ's image.

5. Expository preaching provides variety to sustain a congregation's interest
from week to week. If variety is the spice of life, then the pulpit needs to show it

by a preaching style that reflects something of a great journey, with ever-changing landscapes and challenges.

What makes Tolkien's epic Lord of the Rings so utterly spellbinding is the sheer variety of its style. Moments of intense drama are interspersed with slow-moving developments of character and background. The latter is indispensable for the former, and, indeed, without those less-hurried moments, the dramatic sections would lose their power. Suddenly dipping into the journey through the Mines of Moria to the Bridge at Khazad-dûm would make no sense unless we had journeyed with the hobbits all the way from Rivendell and, indeed, from Hobbiton itself.

Not every sermon should be explosive in nature, and it is only in the discipline of consecutive expository preaching that the necessary elements can be set in place for the drama and excitement of certain passages to have their intended effect.[50]

6. Expository preaching, better than any method I know, aids preachers in thinking and preparing ahead. Not only does it free preachers from the tyranny of having to choose a text (and then choosing another, and then another, when the text fails to yield to the preacher's tapping![51]), it enables him to think well ahead. Certain themes can receive greater and lesser emphasis if the preacher knows that an occasion will come again soon, in the next chapter perhaps, for a more sustained examination of them. Every book of the Bible contains passages which are "hard to understand" (2 Peter 3:16), and preparation for these can take place well in advance.

Faithful expository preaching, whether textual or consecutive, is "a most exacting discipline," according to Stott. He adds:

> Perhaps that is why it is so rare. Only those will undertake it who are prepared to follow the example of the apostles and say, "It is not right that we should give up preaching the Word of God and serve tables. . . . We will devote ourselves to prayer and to the ministry of the Word" (Acts 6:2, 4). The systematic preaching of the Word is impossible without the systematic study of it. It will not be enough to skim through a few verses in daily Bible reading, nor to study a passage only when we have to preach from it. No. We must daily soak ourselves in the Scriptures. We must not just study, as through a microscope, the linguistic minutiae of a few verses, but take

out our telescope and scan the wide expanses of God's Word, assimilating its grand theme of divine sovereignty in the redemption of mankind. "It is blessed," wrote C. H. Spurgeon, "to eat into the very soul of the Bible until, at last, you come to talk in Scriptural language, and your spirit is flavoured with the words of the Lord, so that your blood is Bibline and the very essence of the Bible flows from you."[52]

Commenting upon the preaching of Dr. Martyn Lloyd-Jones, J. I. Packer writes:

> I have never known anyone whose speech communicated such a sense of the reality of God as did the Doctor in those occasional moments of emphasis and doxology. Most of the time, however, it was clear, steady analysis, reflection, correction and instruction, based on simple thoughts culled from the text, set out in good order with the minimum of extraneous illustration or decoration. He knew that God's way to the heart is through the mind (he often insisted that the first thing the gospel does to a man is to make him think), and he preached in a way designed to help people think and thereby grasp truth—and in the process be grasped by it, and so be grasped by the God whose truth it is.[53]

In the end, that is what we desperately need today: preaching that unpacks the Bible's message and conveys a sense of the reality of God's presence. In the end, only faithful *expository* preaching can do that.

Endnotes

[1] *Westminster Confession of Faith* (Glasgow: Free Presbyterian Publications, 1994), 379.

[2] William Perkins, *The Art of Prophesying* (Edinburgh: Banner of Truth Trust, 1996), 9.

[3] All Scripture quotations in this chapter are from the English Standard Version.

[4] James Denney, *The Expositor's Bible*, New Edition, *The Second Epistle to the Corinthians* (London: Hodder & Stoughton, 1916), 97. William Tyndale rendered the verse, "We are not of those who chop and change the Word of God."

[5] A New Testament *hapax legomenon*, W. F. Arndt and F. W. Gingrich render *orthotomeo* "to guide the word of truth along a straight path." Arndt and Gingrich, *A Greek-English Lexicon of the New Testament and Other Early Christian Literature*, 4th ed. (Chicago: The University of Chicago Press, [1957] 1974), 584.

6 Alec Motyer, foreword to the British edition of Haddon Robinson's *Expository Preaching: Principles and Practice* (Leicester: Inter-Varsity Press, 1980), vi.

7 John Calvin, *Calvin's New Testament Commentaries: The Second Epistle of Paul to the Corinthians, and the Epistles to Timothy, Titus and Philemon*, trans. T. A. Small, eds. David W. Torrance and Thomas F. Torrance (Grand Rapids: Eerdmans, 1991), 330.

8 John Calvin, *Sermons on Deuteronomy*, facsimile edition of 1583 (Edinburgh: Banner of Truth Trust, 1987), 292, Column 1. The sermon is the 49th on Deuteronomy. The Elizabethan spelling has been updated for our purposes here. Cf. T. H. L. Parker, *Calvin's Preaching* (Louisville, Ky.: Westminster/John Knox Press, 1992), 81.

9 See *The Institutes of the Christian Religion*, ed. John T. McNeill, trans. Ford Lewis Battles (Philadelphia: The Westminster Press, 1975), 4.8.6. For other examples, see David L. Puckett, *John Calvin's Exegesis of the Old Testament* (Louisville, Ky.: Westminster Press/John Knox, 1995), 26–27.

10 Calvin, *Institutes of the Christian Religion*, 1.8.2.

11 Theodore Beza, *The Life of John Calvin*, ed. Gary Sanseri (reprint of Calvin Translation Society, 1844, ed. and trans. Henry Beveridge) (Milwaukee, Ore.: Back Home Industries, 1996), 100.

12 Chrysostom was known in the sixth century by the term *chrysostomos*, or "golden-mouthed."

13 Parker, *Calvin's Preaching*, 60.

14 Bryan Chapell, *Christ-Centered Preaching: Redeeming the Expository Sermon* (Grand Rapids: Baker, 1994). In 1992, Chapell produced the now-revised work on sermon illustrations, *Using Illustrations to Preach with Power* (Wheaton, Ill.: Crossway, [1992] 2001).

15 Chapell, *Christ-Centered Preaching*, 129. Robinson's equally well-known definition still has force: "Expository preaching is the communication of a biblical concept, derived from and transmitted through a historical, grammatical, and literary study of a passage in its context, which the Holy Spirit first applies to the personality and experience of the preacher, then through the preacher, applies to the hearers." (Haddon Robinson, *Biblical Preaching: The Development and Delivery of Expository Messages* 2nd ed. [Grand Rapids: Baker, (1980) 2001], 21). In the nineteenth century, William Taylor defined it in simpler form this way: "By expository preaching, I mean that method of pulpit discourse which consists in the consecutive interpretation, and practical enforcement, of a book of sacred canon." (*The Ministry of the Word* [Grand Rapids: Baker, 1975], 155). My own favorite definition comes from Alan M. Stibbs' little book, *Expounding God's Word* (London: Inter-Varsity Press, [1960] 1970), where he writes: "The business of the preacher is to stick to the passage chosen and to set forth exclusively what it has to say or suggest, so that the ideas expressed and the principles enunciated during the course of the sermon plainly come out of the Written Word of God, and have its authority for their support rather than just the opinion or the enthusiasm of their human expositor" (17).

16 The words come from his "Hints on Writing Sermons," in *Let Wisdom Judge*, ed. Arthur Pollard (London: Inter-Varsity Press, 1959), 22. This, he adds, is best done by way of "perpetual application."

17 John MacArthur, Jr. and the Master's Seminary Faculty, *Rediscovering Expository Preaching*, ed. Richard L. Mayhue and Robert L. Thomas (Dallas: Word, 1992), 23.

18 Ibid., 29.

19 D. Martyn Lloyd-Jones, *Preaching and Preachers* (Grand Rapids: Zondervan, 1971).

20 Ibid., 66–67.

21 James Montgomery Boice, *Romans: An Expositional Commentary* (Grand Rapids: Baker, 1995).

22 James Montgomery Boice, *The Gospel of John: An Expositional Commentary* (Grand Rapids: Zondervan, 1985).

23 James Montgomery Boice, *Genesis: An Expositional Commentary* (Grand Rapids: Baker, 1988).

24 James Montgomery Boice, *The Psalms: An Expositional Commentary* (Grand Rapids: Baker, 1994).

[25] James Montgomery Boice, *The Minor Prophets: An Expositional Commentary* (Grand Rapids: Zondervan, 1983).

[26] James Montgomery Boice, *Acts: An Expository Commentary* (Grand Rapids: Baker, 1997).

[27] James Montgomery Boice, *Ephesians: An Expositional Commentary* (Grand Rapids: Baker, 1997).

[28] James Montgomery Boice, *Philippians: An Expositional Commentary* (Grand Rapids: Baker, 2000).

[29] John Owen, *The Works of John Owen*, ed. William H. Gould, 16 vols. (London: Banner of Truth Trust, 1972). There is also the recent translation from the Latin of his *Biblical Theology* (Morgan, Pa.: Soli Deo Gloria, 1994), and the seven-volume commentary on Hebrews, *An Exposition of the Epistle to the Hebrews* (Grand Rapids: Baker, 1980).

[30] The sermons have recently been reprinted in 12 volumes jointly by Dust and Ashes Publications and Reformed Heritage Books (2001) and contain an endorsement to their perennial value by me!

[31] The first volume, on Romans 3:20–4:25, appeared in 1970, and since then another eleven volumes have appeared. They are published by the Banner of Truth Trust.

[32] Lloyd-Jones' "sermons" were delivered on a Friday evening rather than on Sundays, a fact that many imitators failed to observe. The audience, therefore, was very different, comprising ardent and enthusiastic admirers of "the Doctor's" preaching style. Some traveled long distances every week in order to be there. Though they comprise some of the finest preaching on Romans ever to have been done, it is doubtful whether most preachers have the gifting to mimic it.

[33] J. C. Ryle, *The Upper Room* (London: Banner of Truth Trust, [1888] 1970), 42. Cf. J. I. Packer, *Faithfulness and Holiness: The Witness of J. C. Ryle* (Wheaton, Ill.: Crossway, 2002), 62.

[34] The complete set was published by Pilgrim Publications (Pasadena, Texas) in 1977.

[35] Only Charles H. Spurgeon could preach on the phrase "until he find it" in Luke 15:4, for example! The sermon was preached on Thursday evening, June 28, 1877, and can be found in volume 49 of his collected sermons.

[36] Sidney Greidanus, *The Modern Preacher and the Ancient Text* (Grand Rapids and Leicester: Eerdmans and Inter-Varsity Press, 1996).

[37] This is *not* a criticism of systematic theology. After all, I am gainfully employed teaching systematic theology to seminary students and happen to think that Berkhof is essential reading. Louis Berkhof, *Systematic Theology* (Edinburgh: Banner of Truth Trust, [1939] 1971).

[38] See Donald Macleod, "Preaching and Systematic Theology," in *The Preacher and Preaching: Reviving the Art in the Twentieth Century* (Phillipsburg, N.J.: Presbyterian & Reformed, 1986), 246–274, and J. I. Packer, "The Preacher as Theologian," in *When God's Voice Is Heard: Essays on Preaching Presented to Dick Lucas*, ed. Christopher Green and David Jackman (Leicester: Inter-Varsity Press, 1995), 79–96. See also Sinclair B. Ferguson's essay, "The Preacher as Theologian," in *The Practical Preacher: Practical Wisdom for the Pastor-Preacher* (Fern, Ross-shire: Christian Focus, 2002), 103–115.

[39] See John R. W. Stott, *Between Two Worlds: The Challenge of Preaching Today* (Grand Rapids: Eerdmans, [1982] 1994).

[40] Westminster Confession of Faith, I.7.

[41] Though dated, John A. Broadus' justly famous work on homiletics is still of enormous value. *A Treatise on the Preparation and Delivery of Sermons*, 2nd ed. (London: James Nisbet & Co., 1871). He has some useful things to say about expository preaching on pages 299–318.

[42] J. W. Alexander, *Thoughts on Preaching* (Edinburgh: Banner of Truth Trust, [1864] 1975), 237.

[43] Taylor, *The Ministry of the Word*, 161.

[44] Part 1 of the trilogy *The Lord of the Rings* by J. R. R. Tolkien.

[45] Cf. Sinclair B. Ferguson, "Exegesis," in *The Preacher and Preaching*, ed. Samuel T. Logan, Jr. (Phillipsburg, N.J.: Presbyterian & Reformed, 1986), 210.

[46] R. L. Dabney, *Lectures on Sacred Rhetoric* (Edinburgh: Banner of Truth Trust, 1870), 81. The book now appears under the title *Evangelical Eloquence: A Course of Lectures on Preaching* (Edinburgh: Banner of Truth Trust, 1999).

[47] "Rehabilitating Discipleship: An Interview with John Stott," in *Prism*, July-August 1995. Cited in *John Stott: A Biography. The Later Years*, by Timothy Dudley-Smith (Downers Grove, Ill.: InterVarsity, 2001), 335.

[48] Cf. Alexander, *Thoughts on Preaching*, 234–235.

[49] Again, Dabney is succinct when he suggests that "the expository method enables the pastor to introduce without offence those delicate subjects of temptation and duty, and those obnoxious doctrines and rebukes, which, on the opposite method, always incur so much *odium*. The fragmentary preacher will find it a very difficult and delicate thing to request his charge to give him the Sabbath hour for the discussion of polygamy, of divorce, or of other sins against chastity." (*Lectures on Sacred Rhetoric*, 83–84.)

[50] Dabney is again pertinent: "The expository method is also naturally adapted to sustain the interest of common minds, in that it provides them with frequent and easy transitions of subject. To be held long to the contemplation of the same abstract thought is exceedingly irksome to them." (Ibid., 87.)

[51] I sometimes liken sermon outlining to a certain chocolate product in the shape of an orange that needs to be "tapped" on a hard surface for the segments to fall apart.

[52] John R. W. Stott, *The Preacher's Portrait* (Grand Rapids: Eerdmans, 1961), 30–31.

[53] J. I. Packer, "David Martyn Lloyd-Jones," in *Collected Shorter Writings of J. I. Packer* (Carlisle, U.K.: Paternoster, 1999), 4:85.

Chapter 4

■ ■ ■

EXPERIENTIAL PREACHING

Joel R. Beeke

*W*hile I was on active duty in the U.S. Army Reserves, a sergeant laid his hand on my shoulder one day and said, "Son, if you ever have to go to war, there are three things you must remember in battle: what tactics you need to use, how the fight is going (which is usually very different from how it ought to be going), and the goal of the battle." With those words, that sergeant gave me an experiential approach to fighting. And his three points provide insight into the process of experiential religion and preaching.

There are five questions I would like to consider as we address the important subject of Reformed experiential preaching:

1. What is experiential religion and preaching?
2. Why is the experiential aspect of preaching necessary?
3. What are the essential characteristics of experiential preaching?
4. Why must a minister habitually exhibit holiness to be effective in the ministry?
5. What practical lessons on Christian living can we learn from the experiential preaching of our predecessors?

Defining Experiential Religion and Preaching

Experiential (or "experimental") preaching addresses the vital matter of how a Christian experiences the truth of Christian doctrine in his life. The term *experimental* comes from the Latin *experimentum*, meaning trial. It is derived from the verb *experior*, meaning "to try, prove, or put to the test." That same verb can also mean "to find or know by experience," thus leading to the word *experientia*, meaning knowledge gained by experiment. John Calvin used the terms *experiential* and *experimental* interchangeably, since both words in biblical preaching indicate the need for measuring experienced knowledge against the touchstone of Scripture.

Experiential preaching stresses the need to know by experience the great truths of the Word of God. A working definition of experiential preaching might be: "Preaching that seeks to explain in terms of biblical truth how matters ought to go, how they do go, and the goal of the Christian life." Such preaching aims to apply divine truth to the whole range of the believer's personal experience, including his relationships with family, the church, and the world around him.

Paul Helm writes about such preaching:

> The situation [today] calls for preaching that will cover the full range of Christian experience, and a developed experimental theology. The preaching must give guidance and instruction to Christians in terms of their actual experience. It must not deal in unrealities or treat congregations as if they lived in a different century or in wholly different circumstances. This involves taking the full measure of our modern situation and entering with full sympathy into the actual experiences, the hopes and fears, of Christian people.[1]

Experiential preaching is discriminatory. It clearly defines the difference between a Christian and a non-Christian, opening the kingdom of heaven to one and shutting it against the other. Discriminatory preaching offers the forgiveness of sins and eternal life to all who by a true faith embrace Christ as Savior and Lord, but it also proclaims the wrath of God and His eternal condemnation upon those who are unbelieving, unrepentant, and unconverted. Such preaching teaches that unless our religion is experiential, we will perish—not because experience itself saves, but because the Christ who saves sinners must be experienced personally as the foundation upon which our lives are built (Matt. 7:22–27; 1 Cor. 1:30; 2:2).

Experiential preaching is applicatory. It applies the text to every aspect of a listener's life, promoting a religion that is truly a power and not a mere form (2 Tim. 3:5). Robert Burns defined such religion as "Christianity brought home to men's business and bosoms," and said the principle on which it rests is "that Christianity should not only be known, and understood, and believed, but also felt, and enjoyed, and practically applied."[2]

Experiential preaching, then, teaches that the Christian faith must be experienced, tasted, and lived through the saving power of the Holy Spirit. It stresses the knowledge of scriptural truth that is able "to make thee wise unto salvation through faith which is in Christ Jesus" (2 Tim. 3:15).[3] Specifically, such preaching teaches that Christ, who is the living Word (John 1:1) and the very embodiment of the truth, must be experientially known and embraced. It proclaims the need for sinners to experience who God is in His Son. As John 17:3 says, "And this is life eternal, that they might know thee, the only true God, and Jesus Christ, whom thou hast sent." The word *know* in this text, as well as in other biblical usages, does not indicate casual acquaintance, but a deep, abiding relationship. For example, Genesis 4:1a uses the word *know* to suggest marital intimacy: "And Adam knew Eve his wife; and she conceived, and bare Cain." Experiential preaching stresses the intimate, personal knowledge of God in Christ.

Such knowledge is never divorced from Scripture. According to Isaiah 8:20, all of our beliefs, including our experiences, must be tested against the Bible. That is really what the word *experimental*, derived from *experiment*, intends to convey. Just as a scientific experiment involves testing a hypothesis against a body of evidence, so experimental preaching involves examining experience in the light of the teaching of the Word of God.

Reformed experiential preaching, grounded in the Word of God, is theocentric rather than anthropocentric. Some people accuse the Puritans of being man-centered in their passion for godly experience. But as J. I. Packer argues, the Puritans were not interested in tracing the experience of the Spirit's work in their souls to promote their own experience, but to be driven out of themselves into Christ, in whom they could then enter into fellowship with the triune God.

This passion for fellowship with the triune God means that experiential preaching not only addresses the believer's conscience, but also his relationship with others in the church and the world. If experiential preaching led me only to examine my experiences and my relationship with God, it would fall short of affecting my interaction with family, church members, and society. It would remain self-centered. True experiential preaching brings a believer into the realm of vital Christian experience, prompting a love for God and His glory as well as a burning passion to declare and display that love to others around him. A believer so instructed cannot help but be evangelistic, since vital experience and a heart for missions are inseparable.

In sum, Reformed experiential preaching addresses the entire range of Christian living. With the Spirit's blessing, its mission is to transform the believer in all that he is and does so that he becomes more and more like the Savior.

Many Reformed ministers preached experientially until early in the 19th century. Francis Wayland wrote in 1857 in his *Notes on the Principles and Practices of the Baptist Churches*:

> From the manner in which our ministers entered upon the work, it is evident that it must have been the prominent object of their lives to convert men to God. They were remarkable for what was called experimental preaching. They told much of the exercises of the human soul under the influence of the truth of the gospel. The feeling of a sinner while under the convicting power of the truth; the various subterfuges to which he resorted when aware of his danger; the successive applications of truth by which he was driven out of all of them; the despair of the soul when it found itself wholly without a refuge; its final submission to God, and simple reliance on Christ; the joys of the new birth and the earnestness of the soul to introduce others to the happiness which it has now for the first time experienced; the trials of the soul when it found itself an object of reproach and persecution among those whom it loved best; the process of sanctification; the devices of Satan to lead us into sin; the mode in which the attacks of the adversary may be resisted; the danger of backsliding, with its evidences, and the means of recovery from it . . . these remarks show the tendency of the class of preachers which seem now to be passing away.[4]

How different experiential preaching is from what we so often hear today! The Word of God is too often preached in a way that will not transform listeners because it fails to discriminate and fails to apply. Such preaching is reduced to a lecture or a demonstration as the preacher caters to what people want to hear. Or it is the kind of subjectivism that is divorced from the foundation of Scripture. Such preaching fails to explain from the Bible what the Reformed called "vital religion":

how a sinner must be stripped of his righteousness, driven to Christ alone for salvation, and led to the joy of simple reliance upon Christ. It fails to show how a saint encounters the plague of indwelling sin, battles against backsliding, and gains victory by faith in Christ.

By contrast, when God's Word is preached experientially, it is "the power of God unto salvation" (Rom. 1:16) that transforms men, women, and nations. This is because such preaching proclaims from the gates of hell, as it were, that those who are not born again will walk through those gates to dwell there eternally unless they repent (Luke 13:1–9). And such preaching proclaims from the gates of heaven that those who by God's grace persevere in holiness will walk through those gates into eternal glory, where they will dwell in unceasing communion with the triune God.

Such preaching is transforming because it accurately reflects the vital experience of the children of God (cf. Rom. 5:1–11), clearly explains the marks of saving grace (Matt. 5:3–12; Gal. 5:22–23), and sets before believer and unbeliever alike their eternal futures (Rev. 21:1–9).

The Necessity of Experiential Preaching

Preaching today must be experiential for the following reasons:

1. *Scripture commands it.* Preaching is rooted in grammatical and historical exegesis, but also involves spiritual, practical, and experimental application. In 1 Corinthians 2:10–16, Paul says that good exegesis is spiritual. Since the Spirit always testifies of Jesus Christ, sound exegesis finds Christ not only in the new covenant, but also in the old. As all roads in the ancient world once led to Rome, so the preaching of all texts today must lead ultimately to Christ. Jesus Himself said, "Search the Scriptures; for in them ye think ye have eternal life: and they are they which testify of me" (John 5:39). Likewise, when He spoke with the travelers to Emmaus, Jesus said, "These are the words which I spake unto you, while I was yet with you, that all things must be fulfilled, which were written in the law of Moses, and in the prophets, and in the psalms, concerning me" (Luke 24:44). Spiritual exegesis is thus christological exegesis, and, through Christ, it will be theological exegesis, bringing all glory to God.

Exegesis offers sound analysis of the words, grammar, syntax, and the historical setting of Scripture. Exposition alone, however, is not true preaching. A minister who presents only the grammatical and historical meaning of God's Word may be lecturing or discoursing, but he isn't preaching. Experiential preaching, while not minimizing the importance of sound interpretive work (words, grammar, syntax, historical background), goes farther. It applies the Word. This application is an essential characteristic of Reformed preaching. Without it, vitality is quenched.

Jesus shows us how to preach experientially in the Sermon on the Mount. He begins the sermon by describing the true citizens of the kingdom of heaven. These verses (Matt. 5:2–11), known as the Beatitudes, are a beautiful summary of the Christian experience. The first three Beatitudes (blessings on those who are poor in spirit, those who mourn, and the meek) focus on the inward disposition of the believer; the fourth (a blessing on those who hunger and thirst after righteousness) reveals the heartbeat of experiential faith; and the last four (blessings on those who are merciful, pure in heart, peacemakers, and persecuted) show faith in the midst of the world. Collectively, the Beatitudes thus reveal the marks of genuine piety. The remainder of Jesus' sermon explains the fruits of grace that inevitably blossom in a believer's life.

2. *True religion is more than intellectual belief.* Because true religion is experiential, preaching must relate to the vital experience of the children of God. Consider the experience of affliction. Romans 5:3–5a says, "We glory in tribulations also: knowing that tribulation worketh patience; and patience, experience; and experience, hope: and hope maketh not ashamed." In this passage, Paul regards experience as an important link to the blessings that flow out of sanctified affliction.

Paul's epistles are filled with experiential truth. Romans 7, for example, shows that human depravity forces a believer to groan, "O wretched man that I am!" (v. 24), and Romans 8 leads a believer to the heights of divine riches in Christ, which the Spirit reveals in all its comfort and glory. Paul concludes by saying that nothing we experience in this life can separate believers from the love of God in Christ Jesus.

Experiential preaching shows both the comfort which belongs to the living church and the glory of God. How could a minister preach the opening words of Isaiah 40 without an experiential emphasis? "Comfort ye, comfort ye my people, saith your God. Speak ye comfortably to Jerusalem, and cry unto her, that her warfare is accomplished, that her iniquity is pardoned: for she hath received of the Lord's hand double for all her sins" (vv. 1–2). A non-experiential sermon fails to offer life and power and comfort to the believer. It also fails to glorify God as Isaiah so eloquently does in the remainder of the chapter.

3. *Without such preaching, we will everlastingly perish.* Experience itself does not save. We cannot have faith in an experience or faith in our faith; our faith is in Christ alone. However, that faith is experiential. Unless we build on the Rock of Christ Jesus (Matt. 7:22–27), our lives ultimately will crash. Some preachers may not know what it means experientially to build their lives upon that Rock. Yet if they are to lead others to Christ, they above all must understand experientially what Paul declares in 1 Corinthians: "But of Him [God the Father] are ye in Christ Jesus, who of God is made unto us wisdom, and righteousness, and sanctification, and redemption. . . . For I determined not to know any thing among you, save Jesus Christ, and Him crucified" (1:30; 2:2).

Characteristics of Experiential Preaching

Experiential preaching includes the following characteristics:

1. *God's Word is central to it.* Preaching flows out of the scriptural passage that is expounded in accord with sound exegetical and hermeneutical principles. As Jeremiah 3:15 says, God has given preachers to His people to feed them "with knowledge and understanding." Proper preaching does not add an experiential aspect to the text being preached; rather, with the Spirit's light, it draws the true experience of believers from the text. The minister must bring the sincere milk of the Word in order that, by the Spirit's blessing, experiential preaching will foster true growth (1 Peter 2:2; Rom. 10:14).

Centering on the Word preserves experiential preaching from unbiblical mysticism. Mysticism separates experience from the Word of God, whereas historic Reformed conviction demands Word-centered, God-glorifying, Spirit-wrought, experiential Christianity. That kind of preaching is essential to the health and prosperity of the church. God begets and multiplies His church only by means of His Word (James 1:18).

2. *It is discerning.* A faithful minister rightly divides the Word of truth to separate the precious from the vile (Jer. 15:19), emphasizing law and gospel, as well as death in Adam and life in Christ. Grace is to be offered indiscriminately to all (Matt. 13:24–30); however, the divine acts, marks, and fruits of grace that God

works in His people must be explained to encourage the elect and uncover the false hopes of the hypocrite.

Biblical experiential preaching stresses what God does in, for, and through His elect. As Philippians 2:13 says, "For it is God which worketh in you both to will and to do of His good pleasure." Expounding the divine acts, marks, and fruits of grace is critical in our day, when so much that is man-glorifying passes for genuine Christianity. We must preach about the fruits of grace that distinguish true belief from counterfeit Christianity. We must be obedient to 2 Corinthians 13:5, which says, "Examine yourselves, whether ye be in the faith; prove your own selves," as well as to James 2:17, which says, "Faith, if it hath not works, is dead, being alone."

3. *It explains how things go in the lives of God's people and how they ought to go.* Telling how matters go without indicating how they should go lulls the believer into ceasing from pressing on in his spiritual pilgrimage. He will not press forward to grow in the grace and knowledge of Christ (2 Peter 3:18). Telling how matters should be rather than how they are discourages the believer from being assured that the Lord has ever worked in his heart. He may fear that the marks and fruits of grace are too high for him to claim. The true believer thus needs to hear both. He must be encouraged in spite of all his infirmities not to despair for Christ's sake (Heb. 4:15). He must also be warned against assuming that he has reached the end of his spiritual pilgrimage and be urged to "press toward the mark for the prize of the high calling of God in Christ Jesus" (Phil. 3:14).

Every Christian is a fighting soldier. To win the war against evil, a believer must put on the whole armor of God (Eph. 6:10–20). Experiential preaching brings the believer to the battlefield, shows him how to fight the war, tells him how to win battles, and reminds him of the ultimate victory that awaits him, a victory in which God will receive all the glory. "For of Him, and through Him, and to Him are all things, to whom be glory for ever. Amen" (Rom. 11:36).

4. *It stresses inward knowledge.* The old divines were fond of stressing the difference between head knowledge and heart knowledge in Christian faith. Head knowledge is not enough for true religion; it also demands heart knowledge. "Keep thy heart with all diligence; for out of it are the issues of life," says Proverbs 4:23. Romans 10:10 adds, "For with the heart man believeth unto righteousness."

Consider the minister who went to a Christian bookstore where a book he had written was being sold. The storekeeper asked the minister whether he knew the book's author. When the man said yes, the storekeeper said that he also was acquainted with the author. The minister disputed that. The storekeeper looked puzzled and asked why he was being questioned. The minister replied, "Sir, if you knew the author, you would have greeted me as such when I entered your store!"

The storekeeper's acquaintance with the author was mere head knowledge. Despite his claims, he did not truly know the author; he didn't even recognize the man when he met him. His knowledge of the author was not experiential; it was not the fruit of personal communion with the author. It lacked the kind of heart knowledge that would have made it authentic.

Heart knowledge of God in Christ results from a personal, experiential encounter with Christ through the wondrous work of the Spirit. Such knowledge transforms the heart and bears heavenly fruit. It savors the Lord and delights in Him (Job 34:9; Ps 34:7; Isa. 58:14). It tastes and sees that God in Christ loves lost, depraved, hell-worthy sinners (Ps. 34:8). Heart knowledge includes an appetite for tasting and digesting God's truth. As Jeremiah says, "Thy words were found, and I did eat them; and Thy word was unto me the joy and rejoicing of mine heart" (Jer. 15:16). Heart knowledge feasts on God, His Word, His truth, and His Son (Pss. 144:15; 146:5).

Heart knowledge does not lack head knowledge, but head knowledge may lack heart knowledge (Rom. 10:8–21). Some people pursue religion as an objective study or to appease their consciences, without ever allowing it to penetrate their hearts. They have understood themselves to be guilty and condemned before the holy justice of God. They have not experienced deliverance in Christ, so they are unaware of the kind of gratitude for such deliverance that masters a believer's soul, mind, and strength. By contrast, those who experience saving heart knowledge find sin such an unbearable burden that Christ is altogether necessary. The grace of deliverance through the Savior is then so overwhelming that their lives shine forth with gratitude.

Head knowledge is not evil in and of itself. Most of our Reformed and Puritan forefathers were highly educated. The Reformers never tired of stressing the value of Christian education. But this education must be animated by the Holy Spirit and applied to the heart (2 Cor. 3:14–18). Head knowledge is insufficient without the Spirit's application to the inward man.

5. It is centered in Jesus Christ (John 1:29, 36). According to 1 Corinthians 2:2, a true preacher must be "determined not to know anything . . . save Jesus Christ, and Him crucified." As William Perkins once said, the heart of all preaching is "to preach one Christ, by Christ, to the praise of Christ."[5]

Christ must be the beginning, middle, and end of every sermon (Luke 24:27; Acts 5:5, 35; 1 John 1:1–4). Preaching must exalt Christ for awakening, justifying, sanctifying, and comforting sinners (Eph. 5:4; 1 Cor. 1:30; Isa. 61:2). As John says, "In him was life; and the life was the light of men. . . . The word was made flesh, and dwelt among us, and we beheld his glory, the glory as of the only begotten of the Father, full of grace and truth" (John 1:4, 14; cf. Pss. 36:9; 119:130).

Experiential preaching must stress what Rowland Hill calls the "three R's" of preaching: ruin by the fall, righteousness by Christ, and regeneration by the Spirit.[6] A Christian recognizes his desperation for Christ. Though conviction of sin cannot save us, it is nonetheless critical. Under the Spirit's tutelage, conviction of sin and misery lead us to the Savior, where we cry out, "Give me Jesus else I die." As Martin Luther once said, "Being saved is going lost at Jesus' feet." This clinging to Jesus is not a one-time event; it is the ongoing state of the Christian life (Col. 2:6–7; John 15:4–5).

6. Its aim is to glorify the triune God. Specifically, it aims to exalt the Father's eternal love and good pleasure, Christ's redemptive and mediatorial work, and the Spirit's sanctifying and preserving ministry. The minister's goal in preaching is to help people fall in love with each person of the Trinity. He does this by stressing the God-centered nature of each benefit of salvation: internal calling, regeneration, faith, justification, sanctification, and perseverance. Experiential preaching exalts what is of God and abases what is of man (John 3:30). Knowing the triune God is the marrow of genuine Christian experience (cf. Jer. 9:23–24; John 17:3).

The Vital Importance of Personal Holiness

It is impossible to separate godly, experiential living from true experiential ministry. The sanctification of a minister's heart is not merely ideal; it is absolutely necessary both personally and for his calling as a minister of the gospel.

Scripture says there should be no disparity between the heart, character, and life of a man who is called to proclaim God's Word and the content of the message he proclaims. "Take heed unto thyself, and unto the doctrine; continue in them; for in doing this thou shalt both save thyself, and them that hear thee" (1 Tim. 4:16).

Jesus condemned the Pharisees and scribes for not doing what they proclaimed. He faulted them for the difference between their words and deeds, between what they professionally proclaimed and how they acted in their daily lives. Professional clerics, more than anyone else, should consider the scathing words of Christ: "The scribes and the Pharisees sit in Moses' seat. All therefore whatsoever they bid you observe, that observe and do; but do not ye after their works: for they say, and do not" (Matt. 23:2–3). As ministers, we are called to be as holy in our private relationships with God, in our roles as husbands and fathers at home, and as shepherds among our people as we appear to be in the pulpit. There must be no disjunction between our calling and our living, between our confession and practice.

Scripture says there is a cause-and-effect relationship between the character of a man's life as a Christian and his fruitfulness as a minister (Matt. 7:17–20). A minister's work is usually blessed in proportion to the sanctification of his heart before God. Ministers must therefore seek grace to build the house of God with sound experiential preaching and doctrine, as well as with a sanctified life. Our preaching must shape our lives, and our lives must adorn our preaching. As John Boys wrote, "He doth preach most who doth live best."

We must be what we preach, not only applying ourselves to our texts but applying our texts to ourselves. Our hearts must be transcripts of our sermons.[7] Otherwise, as John Owen warned, "If a man teach uprightly and walk crookedly, more will fall down in the night of his life than he built in the day of his doctrine."[8]

Lessons from Experiential Preachers

The old experimental preachers were masters at applying truth to their own hearts as well as to those of others. Here are some lessons from the divines that will serve ministers well today:

1. *Live close to God.* You can't fake Reformed, experiential living any more than you can fake Reformed, experiential preaching. People see through ministers who try to preach experientially but don't live up to what they preach, so we must live close to God in order to show others that Christianity is real and experiential. For our words and actions to convey godly piety, our very thoughts must pulsate with

that piety which flows only out of a close life with God. "As a man thinketh, so is he" (Prov. 23:7a).

2. Pursue godliness in dependence on the Holy Spirit. The way to godly living is surprisingly simple: we are to walk with God in His appointed way (Micah 6:8), diligently using the means of grace and the spiritual disciplines, and waiting upon the Holy Spirit for blessing. Note that godly living involves both discipline and grace. This emphasis upon duty and grace is fundamental to Reformed, experiential ideas about godly living.[9] As John Flavel wrote, "The duty is ours, though the power be God's. A natural man has no power, a gracious man hath some, though not sufficient; and that power he hath depends upon the assisting strength of Christ."[10]

Likewise, Owen wrote, "It is the Holy Ghost who is the immediate peculiar sanctifier of all believers, and the author of all holiness in them. The Spirit supplies what we lack so that we may press toward the mark of holiness, enabling us as believers to yield obedience to God . . . by virtue of the life and death of Jesus Christ."[11]

The believer then is empowered, as Flavel said, with "a diligent and constant use and improvement of all holy means and duties, to preserve the soul from sin, and maintain its sweet and free communion with God."[12] We also can be encouraged by Owen's advice: "If thou meanest to enlarge thy religion, do it rather by enlarging thy ordinary devotions than thy extraordinary."[13]

Reformed experiential preachers frequently advised listeners to exercise spiritual disciplines that would promote experiential and practical Christian living. Specifically they advised:

• Read Scripture diligently and meditatively (1 Tim. 4:13). Richard Greenham said that we ought to read our Bibles with more diligence than men dig for hidden treasure. Diligence makes the rough places plain, the difficult easy, and the unsavory tasty.[14]

After reading Scripture, we must ask God for light to scrutinize our hearts and lives, then meditate upon the Word. Disciplined meditation on Scripture helps us focus on God. Meditation helps us view worship as a discipline. It involves our mind and understanding as well as our heart and affections. It works Scripture through the texture of the soul. Meditation helps prevent vain and sinful thoughts (Matt. 12:35), and provides inner resources on which to draw (Ps. 77:10–12), including direction for daily life (Prov. 6:21–22). Meditation fights temptation (Ps. 119:11, 15), provides relief in afflictions (Isa. 49:15–17), benefits others (Ps. 145:7), and glorifies God (Ps. 49:3).

• Pray without ceasing. We must sustain the habit of secret prayer if we are to live experientially before God. The only way to learn the art of holy argument with God is to pray. Prayer helps us cling to the altar of God's promises by which we lay hold of God Himself.

Failing to pray is the downfall of many Christians today. "A family without prayer is like a house without a roof, open and exposed to all the storms of heaven," wrote Thomas Brooks. If the giants of church history dwarf us today, perhaps it is because they were such men of prayer. They were possessed with the Spirit of supplication.

We must cling to the refuge of the inner prayer chamber, for here experiential Christianity is either established or broken. We dare not be content with the shell of religion without the inner core of prayer. When we grow drowsy in prayer, we should pray aloud, write down our prayers, or find a quiet place outside to walk and pray. Above all, we must continue to pray.

We should not give up regular times of prayer, but we should also be open to prayer at the slightest impulse. Conversing with God through Christ is our most effective antidote to spiritual backsliding and discouragement. Discouragement not met with prayer is an open sore ripe for infection, whereas discouragement with prayer is a sore lifted to the balm of Gilead.

Keep prayer a priority in your personal and family life. As John Bunyan said, "You can do more than pray after you have prayed, but you cannot do more than pray until you have prayed. Pray often, for prayer is a shield to the soul, a sacrifice to God, and a scourge to Satan."[15]

• Study Reformed experiential literature. Books that promote godly living are a powerful aid to experiential living. Read the spiritual classics, inviting great writers to be your spiritual mentors and friends. The Puritans excel in such writing. "There must scarcely be a sermon, a treatise, a pamphlet, a diary, a history, or a biography from a Puritan pen, which was not in one way or another aimed at fostering the spiritual life," said Maurice Roberts.[16]

Read sound experiential books on various topics to meet a variety of needs. To foster experiential living by remaining sensitized to sin, read Ralph Venning's

The Plague of Plagues or Jeremiah Burroughs' *The Evil of Evils*. To be drawn closer to Christ, read Isaac Ambrose's *Looking Unto Jesus*. To find peace in affliction, read Samuel Rutherford's *Letters*. To gain relief from temptation, read Owen's *Temptation and Sin*. To grow in holiness, read Flavel's *Keeping the Heart*. Read as an act of worship. Read to be elevated into the great truths of God so that you may worship the Trinity in spirit and in truth.

Be selective about what you read, however. Measure all your reading against the touchstone of Scripture. So much of today's Christian literature is froth, riddled with Arminian theology or secular thinking. Time is too precious to waste on nonsense. Read more for eternity than time, more for spiritual growth than professional advancement. Think of John Trapp's warning: "As water tastes of the soil it runs through, so does the soul taste of the authors that a man reads."

Before picking up a book, ask yourself: Would Christ approve of this book? Will it increase my love for the Word of God, help me to conquer sin, offer abiding wisdom, and prepare me for the life to come? Or could I better spend time reading another book?

Speak to others about the good books you read. Conversation about experiential reading promotes experiential living.

• Make right use of the sacraments. God's sacraments complement His Word. Each sign—water, bread, and wine—nourishes belief in Christ and His sacrifice on the cross, which is the basis for experiential living. The sacraments are visible means through which we and Christ commune. They encourage us to be like Christ in all His holiness.

The grace received through the sacraments is no different from that received through the Word. Both convey the same Christ. But as Robert Bruce put it, "While we do not get a better Christ in the sacraments than in the Word, sometimes we get Christ better."[17]

• Commune with believers. "As the communion of saints is in our creed, so it should be in our company," wrote Thomas Watson. That's good advice. The church ought to be a fellowship of caring as well as a community of prayer (1 Cor. 12:7; Acts 2:42). So talk and pray with believers whose godly walk you admire (Col. 3:16). Association promotes assimilation. A Christian who lives in isolation from other believers will fail to receive the blessings as well as the maturity resulting from godly interaction.[18]

• Keep a journal. Keeping thoughtful records of our spiritual journeys can promote godliness. It can help in our meditation and prayer. It can remind us of the Lord's faithfulness and work. It can help us understand and evaluate ourselves. It can help us monitor our goals and priorities as well as maintain other spiritual disciplines.[19]

• Keep the Lord's Day holy. We ought to view the Sabbath as a joyful privilege, not as a tedious burden. This is the day on which we may worship God and practice spiritual disciplines without interruption. As Packer says, "We are to rest from the business of our earthly calling in order to prosecute the business of our heavenly calling."[20]

• Serve others and tell them about Christ. Jesus expects us to evangelize and serve others (Matt. 28:19–20; Heb. 9:14). We are to do so out of obedience (Deut. 13:4), gratitude (1 Sam. 12:24), gladness (Ps. 100:2), humility (John 13:15–16), and love (Gal. 5:13). Serving others may be difficult at times, but we are called to do so, using every spiritual gift that God has granted us (cf. Rom. 12:4–8; 1 Cor. 12:6–11; Eph. 4:7–13). In fact, serving others is one of our greatest rewards as Christians. If the result is watching them draw closer to Christ through the Spirit's blessing upon God's Word and our efforts, what more could we possibly ask? It is a profoundly humbling experience that can only draw us closer to God.

3. *Aim for balanced thinking.* The great Reformed experiential preachers aimed for balance in Christian living in three important ways:

First, they sought to balance the objective and subjective dimensions of Christianity. The objective is the food for the subjective; thus, the subjective is always rooted in the objective. For example, the Puritans stated that the primary ground of assurance is rooted in the promises of God, but those promises must become increasingly real to the believer through the subjective evidences of grace and the internal witness of the Holy Spirit. Without the Spirit's application, the promises of God lead to self-deceit and carnal presumption. On the other hand, without the promises of God and the illumination of the Spirit, self-examination tends to introspection, bondage, and legalism. Objective and subjective Christianity must not be separated.

We must seek to live in a way that reveals Christ's internal presence based on His objective work of active and passive obedience. The gospel of Christ must be proclaimed as objective truth, but it must also be applied by the Holy Spirit and inwardly appropriated by faith. We therefore reject two kinds of religion: one that separates subjective experience from the objective Word, thereby leading to man-centered mysticism; and one that presumes salvation on the false grounds of historical or temporary faith.[21]

Second, they sought to balance the sovereignty of God and the responsibility of man. Nearly all of our Reformed forefathers stressed that God is fully sovereign and man is fully responsible. How that can be resolved logically is beyond our finite minds, but there is no contradiction here. When Charles H. Spurgeon was asked how these two grand, biblical doctrines could be reconciled, he responded that he didn't know that friends needed reconciliation. Our task is not to force a reconciliation of the two in this life, but to keep them in balance and to live accordingly. We must strive for experiential Christianity that does justice both to God's sovereignty and to our responsibility.

Third, they sought to balance doctrinal, experiential, and practical Christianity. Just as experiential preaching must offer a balance of doctrine and application, Christian living involves more than experience. Biblical Christian living is grounded in sound doctrine, sound experience, and sound practice.

4. *Communicate experiential truth to others.* Reformed experiential preachers applied their sermons to every part of life. They applied all of Scripture to the entire man. They were unashamedly doctrinal.

Given these tendencies, we can learn much from them about how to evangelize, such as:

• Speak the truth about God. That seems obvious. But how often do we speak to others about God's majestic being, His Trinitarian personality, and His glorious attributes? How often do we tell others about His holiness, sovereignty, mercy, and love? Do we root our evangelism in a robust biblical theism or do we take our cues from modern evangelism, which approaches God as if He were a next-door neighbor who adjusts His attributes to our needs and desires? How often do we speak to others about how God and His majestic attributes have become experientially real to us?

• Speak the truth about man. Do we talk to others about our depraved nature and our desperate need for salvation in Jesus Christ? Do we communicate that we are no better than they are by nature; that we are all, apart from grace, sinners with a terrible record, which is a legal problem, as well as in possession of bad hearts, which is a moral problem? Do we talk to them about the dreadful character of sin; that sin is something that stems back to our tragic fall in Adam and affects every part of us, so dominating our mind, heart, will, and conscience that we are slaves to it? Do we describe sin as moral rebellion against God? Do we say that the wages of sin is death, now and for all eternity?

• Speak the truth about Christ. Do we present the complete Christ to sinners, not separating His benefits from His person or offering Him as a Savior while ignoring His claims as Lord? Do we offer Christ as the grand remedy for the great malady of sin and repeatedly declare His ability and willingness to save, and His preciousness as the exclusive Redeemer of lost sinners?

Do we exhibit the way of salvation in Christ in our faith and repentance? Paul said, "I testified to you publicly and from house to house repentance toward God, and faith toward our Lord Jesus Christ" (Acts 20:20–21). Do we likewise evangelize our friends and neighbors when God offers that opportunity? Do we explain to them what faith and repentance are?

• Speak the truth about sanctification. Do we tell others how a Christian must walk the King's highway of holiness in gratitude, service, obedience, love, and self-denial? Do we tell how they must learn the art of meditation, of fearing God, and of childlike prayer, how they must press on by God's grace, seeking to make their calling and election sure? Do we disciple our associates in the need for habitual, experiential faith, repentance, and godliness?[22]

• Speak the truth about eternal consequences. Are we afraid to speak about the consequences of despising the blood of Jesus Christ? Do we flinch from describing damnation and hell? As one Puritan wrote, "We must go with the stick of divine truth and beat every bush behind which a sinner hides, until, like Adam who hid, he stands before God in his nakedness."

We must speak urgently to people around us because many are on their way to hell. We must confront sinners with the law and gospel, with death in Adam and life in Christ. Let us use every weapon we can to turn sinners from the road of destruction so that they may, through grace, experience a living, experiential relationship with God in Jesus Christ. We know from Scripture and by experience that an omnipotent Christ can bless our efforts and rescue a dead sinner, divorce him from his sinful lusts, and make him willing to forsake his wicked ways and turn to God, fully resolved to make God his goal and his praise. Acts 5:31 says, "Him hath God exalted with His right hand to be a Prince and a Savior, for to give repentance to Israel, and forgiveness of sins." Praise God for the experience of His amazing grace toward us in Christ!

Endnotes

1   Paul Helm, "Christian Experience," *Banner of Truth*, No. 139 (April 1975): 6.

2   Robert Burns, introduction to *Works of Thomas Halyburton* (London: Thomas Tegg, 1835), xiv–xv.

3   All Scripture quotations in this chapter are from the King James Version.

4   Cited in Iain Murray, *Revival and Revivalism* (Edinburgh: Banner of Truth Trust, 1994), 321–322.

5   William Perkins, *Works of William Perkins* (London: John Legatt, 1613), 2:762.

6   Rowland Hill, quoted in Robert Murray McCheyne, *Memoir and Remains of Robert Murray McCheyne* (Edinburgh and London; Oliphant Anderson & Ferrier, 1984), 357.

7   Gardiner Spring, *The Power of the Pulpit* (repr. Edinburgh: Banner of Truth Trust, 1986), 154.

8   John Owen, *The Works of John Owen*, ed. William H. Goold (repr. Edinburgh: Banner of Truth Trust, 1976), 8:57.

9   Daniel Webber, "Sanctifying the Inner Life," in *Aspects of Sanctification, 1981 Westminster Conference Papers* (Hertford-shire: Evangelical Press, 1982), 44–45.

10 John Flavel, *The Works of John Flavel* (repr. London: Banner of Truth Trust, 1968), 5:424.

11 Owen, *The Works of John Owen*, 3:385–86.

12 Flavel, *The Works of John Flavel*, 5:423.

13 Jeremy Taylor, cited by Andrew A. Bonar in McCheyne, *Memoir and Remains of Robert Murray McCheyne*, 52.

14 *The Works of the Reverend and Faithfull Servant of Iesvs Christ, M. Richard Greenham*, ed. H[enry] H[olland] (London: Felix Kingston for Robert Dexter, 1599), 390.

15 John Bunyan, *Prayer* (repr. Edinburgh: Banner of Truth Trust, 1999), 23ff.

16 Maurice Roberts, "Visible Saints: The Puritans as a Godly People," in *Aspects of Sanctification, 1981 Westminster Conference Papers*, 1–2.

17 See the Westminster Larger Catechism, Questions 161–175, for how to use the sacraments properly.

18 Joel R. Beeke, *Assurance of Faith: Calvin, English Puritanism, and the Dutch Second Reformation* (New York: Peter Lang, 1991), 407–408.

19 Donald S. Whitney, *Spiritual Disciplines for the Christian Life* (Colorado Springs: NavPress, 1991), 196–210.

20 J. I. Packer, *A Quest for Godliness: The Puritan Vision of the Christian Life* (Wheaton, Ill: Crossway Books, 1990), 239; cf. Errol Hulse, "Sanctifying the Lord's Day: Reformed and Puritan Attitudes," in *Aspects of Sanctification, 1981 Westminster Conference Papers*, 78–102.

21 Joel R. Beeke, *The Quest for Full Assurance: The Legacy of Calvin and His Successors* (Edinburgh: Banner of Truth Trust, 1999), 125, 130, 146.

22 Joel R. Beeke, *Puritan Evangelism: A Biblical Approach* (Grand Rapids: Reformation Heritage Books, 1999), 15-16.

Chapter 5

■ ■ ■

THE TEACHING PREACHER

R. C. Sproul

*I*n the mid-twentieth century, a full-length film was made about the life of Martin Luther. It included a scene that I found particularly provocative. The scene took place after Luther's historic meeting with the authorities of the Holy Roman Empire and of the Roman Catholic Church at the Diet of Worms. When Luther was called upon at Worms to recant of his teachings, he made his epic stand, stating: "Unless I am convicted by Scripture and plain reason . . . my conscience is captive to the Word of God. I cannot and I will not recant anything, for to go against conscience is neither right nor safe. Here I stand, I cannot do otherwise. God help me."[1] He then left the assembly hall and was taken on horseback by his friends to Wartburg Castle, there to be hidden and protected from the authorities, who were soon to put a price on his head. At the castle, Luther grew a beard and disguised himself as a knight known as Sir George. Then he set to work on the task of translating the Bible into German.

While Luther was hidden away in the castle, his colleague, Andreas Carlstadt, in his zeal to promote the Reformation, went to churches and smashed stained-glass windows and other pieces of art. It was a reckless work of vandalism in the name of reformation. When word of Carlstadt's destructive activity got back to Luther, he was horrified, for this was not what he intended by the Reformation. Despite the fact that Luther was wanted dead or alive, he got on his horse, left the castle, and came back to the church in Wittenberg. The scene in the movie shows Carlstadt, Philip Melanchthon, and others meeting quietly behind closed doors. Suddenly, Luther enters, dressed as a knight in chain mail. They look at him and ask: "Brother Martin, what are you doing? Why are you here?" Luther replies, "I want my pulpit."

I don't know whether that event actually took place in church history or whether this represented the director's creativity in producing the film, but that scene thrilled me because it captured the spirit of Luther. One of the most significant things about Luther's life is that after the Reformation began and he had become a celebrity throughout Western Europe, he did not spend his time traveling around the Continent trying to consolidate the movement. Rather, he returned to the primary vocation to which he had been ordained. He spent his years teaching and preaching in Wittenberg, just as John Calvin did in Geneva. So when Luther writes and comments about what a preacher should be and about the task of preaching in the church, I listen. Surely we all can be instructed from his insights.

One of the great gifts to the church is a large book titled *What Luther Says*.[2] The corpus of Luther's *Works* consists of fifty-five thick volumes, so I utilize this anthology to survey Luther's writings topically. In this book, one can find collected statements from the various works of Luther regarding the preacher and preaching. What follows is the distilled essence of that collection.

The Preacher: Apt to Teach

The first thing that is required of a preacher, according to Luther, is that he be "apt to teach." At this point, Luther is simply echoing the apostolic qualifications set forth in the New Testament for the position of elder (1 Tim. 3:1–7). The person who is elevated to a position of leadership in the church of God, and is given oversight and supervision of the flock of God, must be able to teach. Luther saw this as the primary task of the minister.

This concept is all but lost in the church today. When we call ministers to our churches, we frequently demand that they be administrators, skilled at fundraising and project management. We also hope that they might know a little bit of theology and a little bit of the Bible, and we expect them to preach interesting and often entertaining sermons. But we often don't make it a priority that pastors be equipped to teach the congregation the things of God.

Not only is this tendency contrary to Luther's admonition, it is against scriptural teaching. Think of Jesus' confrontation of Peter following Peter's three public denials of Jesus:

> So when they had eaten breakfast, Jesus said to Simon Peter, "Simon, son of Jonah, do you love Me more than these?"
>
> He said to Him, "Yes, Lord; You know that I love You."
>
> He said to him, "Feed My lambs."
>
> He said to him again a second time, "Simon, son of Jonah, do you love Me?"
>
> He said to Him, "Yes, Lord; You know that I love You."
>
> He said to him, "Tend My sheep."
>
> He said to him the third time, "Simon, son of Jonah, do you love Me?" Peter was grieved because He said to him the third time, "Do you love Me?"
>
> He said to Him, "Lord, You know all things; You know that I love You."
>
> Jesus said to him, "Feed My sheep." (John 21:15–17)[3]

Three times Jesus instructed the apostle to be engaged in the tending, leading, and feeding of His sheep. Why? It was because the people of God who are assembled in the congregations of churches all over the world belong to Jesus; they are His sheep. Every minister who is ordained is entrusted by God with the care of those sheep. We call the position "the pastorate" or "the pastoral ministry," because the pastor (from the Latin *pastor*, meaning "herdsman" or "shepherd") cares for the sheep of Christ. What shepherd would so neglect his sheep that he would fail to feed them? It is the feeding of the sheep, according to Luther, that is the prime task of the ministry. And that feeding comes, principally, through teaching.

I make a distinction between preaching—which involves exhortation, exposition, admonition, encouragement, and comfort—and teaching, which involves the transfer of information. I practice both in my own ministry, and sometimes I obscure the distinction. The students in my seminary classes will testify that sometimes, in the middle of my lectures, when I'm trying to communicate certain doctrines and information about theology, I'll start preaching, because I'm not interested in the mere transfer of information. I want that information not only to get in their heads but in their bloodstreams. In fact, I warn them at the beginning of each course: "Don't think that I'm in this classroom as a professor in a state of neutrality. I'm after your mind and your heart. I hope not only to instruct you, but to persuade you. I want to move you to grasp not only the truth of this content, but also the importance and the sweetness of it, so that you will take it with you for the rest of your lives. It is not my goal simply to transfer information from my brain to your notebook, because learning doesn't take place until it gets in your head and into your life." Likewise, when I preach, I often sprinkle some conceptual education into the content of my sermons. So I have a tendency to skate back and forth across the line between preaching and teaching. However, I've always thought that the primary thing, as Luther understood, that I'm responsible to do as a minister is to teach the people the things of God.

The Content of Teaching

Here we may well ask Luther: if the top priority of the minister is teaching, what is he to teach? Luther would reply: The Bible, the content of Scripture. Calvin wrote commentaries on almost every book of the Bible, and those commentaries grew out of teaching seminars he gave to his congregation in Geneva. Luther also wrote many commentaries based on his lectures to his congregation and students in Wittenberg. These Reformers gave much of their time and effort to teaching the Bible, and all pastors should do the same.

Some years ago, when I was on the faculty at a theological seminary, we reviewed the curriculum. We asked ourselves: what does a man have to know in order to be a godly pastor? We decided that the main thing was the content of Holy Scripture. So many seminary courses are designed to answer academic questions of background, of authorship, and technical problems that we never get around to the English Bible. Our future ministers are coming out of seminaries not fully conversant with the content of the Bible. So we began to develop a curriculum from ground zero. We said, let's step out of the academic world for a minute and design the curriculum not to train professors in the areas of their specialties, but to serve the church and thereby to serve Christ.

Many ministers are frankly afraid to teach the content of Scripture to the people because they haven't learned it themselves. The people of God need to say to their pastors, or to their prospective pastors, "Feed us the Word of God." Congregations must be careful to choose pastors who will open up the Scriptures to them.

The last months of the year 2000 were a period of mourning for me over the loss of one of my closest friends and comrades in the ministry, Dr. James Montgomery Boice. Jim Boice represented to me the model minister. Here was a man who went to Harvard University for his undergraduate degree, then to Princeton Seminary for his degree for ministry, and from there to the University of Basil in Switzerland for his doctor's degree in New Testament study. He had all the credentials a person could want to go to the top of the ladder in the academic world, but that was not his call. His call was to be a pastor. For more than thirty years he opened the Word of God in his preaching, in his teaching, and in his writings. Fidelity to Scripture drove him, and a more courageous Christian I have never met.

The teaching of the Word is what God expects from those whom He sets apart and ordains as ministers. He desires that they will take His Word and give it to the people.

A Sound Understanding of Scripture

Pastors are expected, according to Luther, to manifest a godly life. Yet when Luther made that comment, he wasn't talking simply about moral virtue. The pastor must be irreproachable in his *doctrine*. Luther wasn't interested in doctrine removed from life. For Luther, doctrine *is* life, because what a person believes determines his behavior. Therefore, the preacher who teaches the Word of God must be sound in his understanding of the sacred Scriptures.

Furthermore, Luther said that the minister needs to be sure of his doctrine. That is a strange quality for a great minister. In this day and age, we tend to put a premium on openness; we don't like the dogmatic spirit of people who are too certain of that which they teach or preach. We almost expect the minister, if he is to be politically correct, to say, "Well, maybe it is this and maybe it is that," because we don't want him to offend anyone by a proclamation that communicates too much certainty or authority. To that, Luther would say, "No, no, no, no." The pastor is responsible to do his homework. He's not supposed to manifest a certitude that is born of arrogance, but one that comes from the text of Scripture itself.

The great Dutch humanist and theologian Desiderius Erasmus initially was a fan of Luther, but he soon came to believe that Luther had gone too far. Thereafter, Erasmus emerged as one of Luther's chief critics, and he wrote a scathing critique of Luther in his book titled *The Diatribe*. Perhaps Luther's most famous written work (and I certainly believe his most important), *The Bondage of the Will*, was written in response to *The Diatribe*. In *The Bondage of the Will*, when Luther was responding to the attacks of Erasmus, he quoted Erasmus as saying that on difficult doctrines such as predestination, election, and issues of freedom of the will and so on, Erasmus preferred to "suspend judgment" and not make assertions. It was Erasmus' view that the proper academic posture of the scholar, when investigating such issues, is to be very cautious, to reserve judgment, and to hesitate from coming to firm conclusions. Erasmus said that he would prefer not to make assertions on such subjects. Luther became apoplectic over this position of Erasmus. He said: "Nothing is more familiar or characteristic among Christians than assertion. Take away assertions, and you take away Christianity."[4] Then, in his passion, Luther said: "Away, now, with Skeptics and Academics from the company of us Christians; let us have men who will assert."[5]

Luther would have none of the spirit of those who are always learning and never coming to a knowledge of the truth (2 Tim. 3:7). The foundational truths of Christianity were built on the blood of the martyrs, because the apostles didn't go into the marketplace saying: "Well, maybe Jesus rose from the dead or maybe He didn't. You need to examine this, and suspend judgment." No, they were bold in their assertions because they knew what they believed (2 Tim. 1:8-12). They understood the things of God, were convinced of the truth of the claims of Jesus, and, having that assurance and certainty of the truthfulness and trustworthiness of Scripture, they went boldly into a dying world. Luther did the same.

For instance, Luther was certain about the doctrine of justification. Without his assurance that the Bible taught that doctrine, he never could have stood against all the authority structures of his day. He wanted and expected the same kind of certainty from every minister—again, not a dogmatic spirit born out of arrogance, but a certainty that is rooted and grounded in a disciplined mastery of the Word of God. Both Luther and Calvin, even to this day, are regarded in the academic world as incredible geniuses who exhibited a rare and extraordinary mastery of their material. That is what ministers are called to achieve. The enterprise of teaching requires nothing less than that kind of due diligence. Why? Because their task is not to spread their opinions, but to set forth with clarity and boldness the Word of God.

A practicing psychologist from San Francisco came to me after a seminar on one occasion. She was very upset with her minister and said: "I've come to the place where I am convinced that our minister is doing everything he possibly can to conceal the real nature of God from us in his preaching. He's afraid that the preaching of the gospel might offend somebody, or that the setting forth of the character of God in His holiness, sovereignty, justice, and wrath will make people uncomfortable and cause them to leave the church. I go to church to hear a word from God, and I'm starving to death in my church." I can't tell you how many telephone calls and letters I get from people who basically echo those sentiments. In desperation, they're crying out to their pastors: "We're not interested in psychoanalysis on Sunday morning. We don't come to church to hear a commentary on the latest political issues in America. If we want that, we can turn on CNN or Fox News. We come to church to hear a word from God. We don't want your opinions. We want to hear a prophetic ministry that prefaces the sermon with the words, 'Thus saith the Lord.'"

This is how Luther and Calvin understood the task of the minister. The greatest awakening in the history of the church took place when, after darkness had eclipsed the truth of the gospel and hidden the Word in obscurity, the light burst forth and awakened Christendom in the sixteenth century. That light was carried to churches by men who saw it as their task to present the unembellished, undiluted, unvarnished Word of God and were bold enough to do just that. So they pored over the texts of Scripture, taking great care in their exegesis before they entered the pulpit. Since that was the center of their task, they were fearless. Their courage came from the conviction that what they were preaching and teaching was the Word of God.

Guarding against False Teaching

In our day, we've seen a revolution in worship that is being driven, in many ways, by an attempt to be winsome to the people of our age. As the culture has become increasingly secular, there has been an attempt to rethink the church, removing all of the artifacts of "churchiness"—pulpits, pews, and hymnals—turning the church building into what looks like a concert hall, and converting worship into an outreach ministry that comes across as exciting, interesting, and "relevant." It's almost as if we're saying to our congregations today, "Let us entertain you."

However, the temptation to turn the pulpit into theater and the church building into a place of entertainment is not a new phenomenon. It was also a problem with which Luther struggled in the sixteenth century. When he preached his most powerful sermons on justification by faith alone, Luther noted that people fell asleep in his congregation. He reckoned that the people in the parishes came to church merely to be entertained. Even in the sixteenth century, during the middle of the Reformation, the pastors were struggling with the demands of their congregations that they entertain them with their preaching. Luther declared that it is not the task of the pastor to entertain, but to nurture and feed the flock in faithfulness to the Word of God. He said it is the task of the minister to protect the flock from heresy and from error. Today, if you preach against heresy and error, you are entering into the arena of the politically incorrect, because we live in a culture that has been captured by the spirit of relativism. Relativism says that truth is what you perceive it to be, and what is true for you may be false for somebody else.

In our society, you're perfectly free to believe whatever you like, but the one thing you may not do is deny its antithesis. You can say, "I believe that this is true." But you cannot say with impunity that that which opposes your belief is false. A whole generation of Christians has been brainwashed by the spirit of relativism, so they're completely hesitant to say, "I deny that error over there." We don't have heresy trials anymore because, in relativism, there is no such thing as heresy.

In the aftermath of the 2000 presidential election, when the Supreme Court was brought in to decide the matter, Justice Sandra Day O'Connor raised a question about voter responsibility. She commented that each voter had directions that told him or her how to operate the voting machines, and that the instructions warned each voter to be sure the stylus penetrated and no loose chads were left hanging. These things were the responsibility of the person who went in to cast a vote. One of the news commentators heard her question and declared that O'Connor was assuming that in America it is a privilege to vote, and that with that privilege comes a corresponding responsibility. But he asked, "Doesn't she understand that in our culture there is no such thing as responsibility?" In a relativistic environment, you can't hold someone responsible for anything.

Even before relativism became fashionable, Luther had to deal with the responsibility of the shepherd to protect his sheep from false teaching. Luther understood that in Old Testament Israel, the greatest threat to the security of the nation was not the armies of the Syrians, the Assyrians, the Babylonians, or the Philistines. The people of Old Testament Israel were crushed by the false prophets within their gates. Jeremiah stood before God saying: "Lord, I quit. I will speak no more in your name. I am in derision daily." Every time Jeremiah opened his mouth to proclaim the Word of God to Jerusalem, a hundred false prophets would answer him by telling the people, "Peace, peace," when there was no peace. The people didn't want to hear the bad news that Jeremiah was prophesying, so they heaped to themselves false teachers. They went to hear the teachers and the preachers who preached what they wanted to hear. When Jeremiah complained about that, God reassured him, saying, "The prophet who has a dream, let him tell a dream; and he who has My word, let him speak My word faithfully" (Jer. 23:28a).

In the metaphor of the sheep, the false prophet was the wolf in sheep's clothing. He was the one who came in and preached in a religious setting to the sheep (i.e., the household of God). The content of that preaching was to the people's everlasting destruction and ruin. The true prophet, one who is a good shepherd, puts his life on the line for his sheep. There is a reason why the shepherd has that rod and staff—they are to protect the sheep from the wolves who would come in to ravage them. Luther said that the false teacher is the worst of all possible criminals, because he spreads a poison that has everlasting consequences. The pastor must protect his sheep from such spiritually criminal behavior.

Finally, Luther said that it is the task of the preacher to defend not his own honor, but the honor of God and Christ. That is where the preacher rises to defend the truth. He does not seek to protect his own opinion or his own reputation, but the truth of God. That is the duty of the pastor, because the honor of God has all but been wiped away in our day, not from outside the church but from inside. I tell my seminary students: "Don't ever, ever, ever, ever preach your own anger. If you're angry about something, recuse yourself from preaching on that issue. Don't ever use the pulpit as your personal soapbox. If you want to proclaim the wrath of God, you'd better make sure it's God's wrath and not your own. You should be clear that your concern is the honor of Christ and not your own honor." Every minister brings his flesh with him into the pulpit. It is a sacred thing to heed the spirit of the Word of God while guarding against the flesh.

The Centrality of Christ in Preaching

For the Reformers, the center of worship was to be the preaching of the Word of God, and the central theme of that preaching, according to Luther, was to be Christ. Luther approached this question with an emphasis on the gospel, but not an exclusive emphasis. He made an important distinction between law and gospel. He was convinced that preachers ought to preach the law as well as the gospel because, unless the law is set forth clearly and unambiguously, people will never have an appreciation for the gospel. In one sense, Luther anticipated where we are today—a time when the gospel has fallen almost into obscurity. People are not excited about the gospel because they tacitly assume that there is no great need for it. We are told that God loves everybody unconditionally; that He accepts us just as we are. If that were true, we would have no need to flee from our guilt and sin to embrace the gospel.

Luther himself was almost completely crushed by his study of the law. During his time in the monastery, he spent hours every day in confession, telling his confessor all the sins he could recall from the previous twenty-four hours. His confessor finally grew frustrated, thinking that if Luther was going to confess sins, he ought to confess something big, not things such as, "I coveted Brother David's morsel of meat on his plate last night" or "I stayed up five minutes past lights-out time reading my Bible by candlelight." What kind of trouble can you get into in a monastery that would take two or three hours to confess the next day?

We must remember that Luther had been educated in jurisprudence. He was a promising student of law before he fled to the monastery for refuge from the wrath of God. So Luther would pore over the biblical law, and he saw the law as a mirror that revealed, on the one hand, the perfect righteousness and holiness of God, and on the other hand, his own lack of righteousness. So if there ever was a person tormented by guilt because of familiarity with the law of God, it was Luther. He said later that before God will allow people to experience the sweetness and joy of heaven, He first dangles them, as it were, over the pit of hell so that they can see what their estate would be apart from the gospel.

Luther also was captured by what Paul calls the pedagogical function of the law. Paul speaks of the law as the divine pedagogue—that is, the schoolmaster who brings us to Christ. That particular metaphor can be a little bit misleading. In the ancient world, there were two adults in the classroom. One would communicate the information necessary for learning; he transferred the content. The other person carried a long stick and was basically the disciplinarian. If students in the classroom misbehaved or got out of line, the disciplinarian would come along and tap them on the shoulder lightly. If the misbehavior became more severe, the disciplinarian would tap less gently. That is what Paul was saying about the function of the law. The law corrects, disciplines, and exposes our evil, and therefore drives us to the gospel.

One of the age-old issues that Augustine dealt with in his interaction with the heretic Pelagius was whether God is unjust in commanding perfection from human beings. Augustine said that we are fallen and dead in sin and trespasses. Therefore, we cannot fulfill God's mandate to be holy even as He is holy (Lev. 11:44; 1 Peter 1:16). Pelagius countered that God would command us to be holy and perfect only if we have the ability in and of ourselves to do so. Pelagius' heresy was categorically rejected by the church on many occasions. However, Luther also wondered why God gave laws He knew we wouldn't be able to fulfill. His answer was that the law has an evangelical function—it is designed to drive us to the gospel.

In the church I pastor, we read from the Ten Commandments each Sunday morning, with a brief exposition of one of them. We do this for the same reason Luther and Calvin agreed upon in the sixteenth century—we must keep the law of God before the people so that they may lay hold of the gospel.

So Luther saw that the task of the preacher is to preach both law and gospel. Never would he allow the possibility of merely preaching the gospel without ever preaching the law. If a pastor preaches nothing except the "good news" and never preaches the "bad news," the good news becomes "no news." It loses its significance for people.

Avoiding Novelties in Preaching

Luther also said that the minister should never preach novelties. The theological world often puts a premium on that which is new and different. Of course, Luther offered brilliant insights, vignettes of discernment into the Word of God that in many ways were exceedingly fresh and helpful in awakening the people of his day. A minister may communicate a vignette of insight drawn from the text itself, something that may have been forgotten or overlooked. But Luther was talking about creative invention. There is no room for that in the pulpit, and there is no room for it in the teaching of the people of God.

One of the problems we have in the church today is that liberal theology has so captured many of the mainline denominations that the ministers no longer teach from the content of Scripture at all. How does that happen historically? It is axiomatic that as the seminaries go, so go the pastors; and as the pastors go, so go the congregations. If you want a reformation, you have to look seriously at what the seminaries are teaching.

Seminaries are academic institutions, and they are always competing for academic respectability. They want the professors with the best credentials from the most acclaimed universities. At the academic level, in order to get a doctorate, you have to publish a doctoral dissertation. In most institutions, in order to qualify for a Ph.D. dissertation, you have to come up with a thesis that is new. So there is a premium on novelty. Of course, it is perfectly fine for somebody engaged in chemical research to discover new insights in terms of how certain chemicals interact. The sciences, particularly the physical sciences, are subject to great advances with further research and novel experimentation. But when it comes to the content of a book that was completed two thousand years ago, one that the best minds in Western history have pored over since then, it is highly unlikely that we will come up with a radically new insight that will change the entire framework for understanding that book. Yet we put pressure on our scholars to do just that.

When I was in graduate school, I read about a student who had received a Ph.D. for a thesis that claimed that there was a particular mushroom that was a hallucinogenic and incited people to all kinds of sexual eroticism, and that Jesus had founded a cult based upon that. That kind of thing is manifestly absurd. One has to completely ignore all of the classical standards of historical research to come up with such a thesis. But in our day, the more novel something is, the more enticing it becomes for academic recognition.

There is a left wing and a right wing in theological scholarship. Not only that, there are radical left and right wings. The lunatic fringe on the left wing is inhabited by people such as those who made up "the Jesus Seminar," a group of scholars that came together in the 1980s to debate the historicity of the Gospel accounts of Jesus' life. People object to my characterization of the Jesus Seminar participants as part of the "lunatic fringe" because they are "scholars." I reply that, though these people have advanced academic degrees, they are utterly irresponsible and they do not practice sober scholarship. I can find myself on the opposite end of the spectrum from a higher-critical liberal scholar but still respect his methodology, his manner of academic research. However, the Jesus Seminar is concerned with things that are novel, which is why it receives so much press. The Jesus Seminar participants are like the philosophers at the Areopagus in Athens, who were interested in hearing Paul because they were always there to discuss what was new. He was teaching something they had never heard before, that someone actually had been raised from the dead, so they wanted to hear what he had to say.

What God expects from a minister of the gospel is the sober, accurate presentation of His Word. We get no style points for novelty from God. In fact, to be novel with the Word of God is to create something that is not a part of the Word of God; it is to add to the Word that which does not belong to it. At that point, we place ourselves dangerously close to the wrath of God. According to Luther, there is no room for novelty; we are to preach the whole counsel of God, both the law and the gospel in all their fullness, with no inventions.

Helping People Get to Heaven

Luther said it is the preacher's task to show people how to get to heaven. Some people, looking at that purpose statement from a twentieth-century perspective, smile and say: "Are you serious, Luther, that the task of the preacher on Sunday morning is to teach people how to get to heaven? Isn't that so 'otherworldly' in its orientation that we lose the application of the Word of God to the present?"

Luther said that the task of the church is profane. He did not mean that we are to be a profane people in the pejorative sense of that word, as it is commonly used in our language today. The etymological roots of *profane* literally mean "out of the temple" or "outside of the temple." Luther meant that the Christian life is to be so strong that we go out of the temple and into the world. By learning how to get to heaven on the vertical plane, we also learn how to be Christ for our neighbor on the horizontal plane, so that, after we come out of church on Sunday morning, we go into the world with the gospel. Luther did not see the task of the church to be contained in a monastery. On the contrary, he envisioned the Word of God penetrating the culture and the strongholds of this world.

That is a far cry from what happened in the nineteenth century, when liberal theology completely denied the importance and value of the vertical relationship. Liberal theologians said Christianity is not about how to get to heaven, but about how to love our neighbor. They said it is not about supernatural reconciliation, but about building a humanitarian society. So the gospel became translated into the so-called "social gospel" of the nineteenth century.

Luther declared that every person's most acute need in life is to be prepared for what happens at the end of that life when he or she dies. The preacher of the Word of God is to prepare every person for making that transition from this world into heaven. As pastors, we are entrusted with the souls of people—their eternal destinies. We live in a day when people don't even believe that we have souls, but the doctrine of the personal continuity of our existence after death is essential to the Christian faith. People need to be prepared for that, and that is the task of the preacher.

One of the reasons ministers try to conjure up new and interesting viewpoints is because they lack confidence in the effectiveness of preaching the whole counsel of God. Luther strongly emphasized that the power of preaching resides not in the preacher or in his technique, but in the power of God as He attends the proclamation of His Word. Of course, Luther understood that the gospel does not belong to the preacher. It doesn't even belong to the church. Paul articulates in Romans 1:1 that he is an apostle separated by God to "the gospel of God." This *of* does not mean "about"; rather, it is *possessive*. When Paul speaks of the gospel of God, he is saying that the gospel belongs to God. He is its Author; He is its Owner. The gospel was not invented by the insights of prophets or preachers, but came from God Himself. So when we proclaim the gospel, we proclaim a message that is not our own.

Later in that same chapter, Paul says that the gospel is the power of God unto salvation for all who believe—that the power is in the gospel, not in our presentation of it. That being the case, it is all the more necessary for the preacher to be careful in how he sets forth the gospel.

Understanding the Gospel

A few years ago at a Christian bookseller's convention, with several thousand people present, one Christian group did a survey asking people to define the gospel.

Out of one hundred responses that were given, only one qualified as an adequate description of the gospel. People think that the gospel is having a warm relationship with Jesus or asking Christ into your heart. Those things are important, but they are not the gospel. The gospel focuses on the person of Christ, what Christ accomplished, and how the benefits of Christ are appropriated to the Christian's life by faith.

Our first task as preachers is to make sure we know the gospel ourselves so that we can proclaim it accurately and boldly. When we do that, it is not our responsibility to make sure that the gospel takes hold in the hearts of men and produces a response of faith. Paul wrote to the Ephesians that we are justified by grace through faith, and that faith is not of ourselves but is the gift of God (Eph. 2:8–9). Even the faith that we hope will be the response to our proclamation of the gospel is not something that we can create; it is a gift from God. So I can preach with the greatest eloquence, the greatest sincerity, with the most modern techniques possible, to multitudes of people, and not see any fruit. Or I can set forth the minimal content of the gospel with very little talent and see a revival break out, because the power is in the gospel as God attends the preaching of His Word. Remember that God has chosen the foolishness of preaching as the means by which He will save the world (1 Cor. 1:20–25).

The Bible puts a premium on the office of preaching. God has chosen the foolishness of preaching as the means for accomplishing His end: the salvation of His people. Luther understood that when he said: "Your task, O preacher, is to make sure that you are faithful to the text, that you are faithful to the proclamation of that gospel, that you are faithful to set forth the whole counsel of God, and then step back and let it happen. I don't have to try to cajole and persuade people with my techniques to get them to respond. I preach the law, I preach the gospel, and the Holy Ghost attends the ministry of that word to bring forth the fruit."

Luther explains that God has entrusted the ministry of the Word to us, not its results, just as He did in the days of Moses, when God sent Moses to Pharaoh. If ever there was a power struggle, it was the confrontation between Moses and Pharaoh, who was the most powerful man in the world at the time. God told Moses, an exile who had been living for years as a lowly shepherd in the Midianite wilderness, to go to Pharaoh and to command him in the name of God to let His people go. Against the forces of this world, Moses was impotent. He had nothing in himself to compare with the power of Pharaoh. But Moses was faithful to deliver God's word to Pharaoh, and God triumphed over Pharaoh and his armies.

The Value of Preaching

For this reason, Luther had a high degree of respect for ministers who were faithful to the Word. He said that the people of God should give high honor and esteem to faithful preachers—even those who are mediocre in their technique.

Americans live in an economy where the marketplace determines the value of goods and services. I can't tell you how valuable your car is to you; only you know that. But we Americans tend to put a high price on automobiles because we're a highly mobile society, and many of us live many miles from our workplaces. We need transportation, so we're willing to spend large amounts in order to have a car. Likewise, we put a premium on our physical health, so we're willing to spend large amounts of money for doctors and medical care.

But watch the cultural habits of people when they go to church. Thirty years ago, the custom was to drop a $1 bill into the collection basket as it was passed. Today the custom is to put a $1 bill in the basket—never mind inflation. If we leave it up to the marketplace, we will find that the lowest-paid professionals in America are teachers and preachers. Why is that? It is because we don't place much value upon the services they provide. That is why, in Old Testament Israel, God commanded a tax upon the people of Israel, the tithe. It was distributed among the Levites, who were responsible for teaching and preaching. God knew that if the value of preaching were left to people, they would never pay for it. Luther classified such a low view of preaching and preachers as a sin against God.

At this point, many churchgoers will say, "We want our preachers to be poor because we don't want them to be worldly." It is never our responsibility to take care of other people's charity; you're responsible for your own charity, not to impose it upon other people. When Luther saw this going on in Germany, he pointed out that even a mediocre preacher is bringing the pearl of great price to the people. Since the minister is handling that which is of eternal, inestimable value, the people ought not to despise his labor.

On the other hand, Luther noted that personal ambition is often a snare for a faithful preacher. You may think that somewhat strange, because you may question why a man would go into the ministry out of personal ambition. One of the attractive things about the ministry is that it gives a person an instant place of leadership over other people. Even if the pay isn't much, the sense of authority and power associated with the pulpit can still be an enticement to people who have no regard for the things of God. Luther cautioned men to be careful of the ambition that can destroy the ministry. He said that the preachers and teachers who are most vulnerable to that destruction are those who are most talented, because they are most vulnerable to pride. Pride becomes the snare to the minister who has something to lose, and he begins to build his own empire rather than being faithful to the things of God.

Aiming for the Heart through the Mind

We do not put our trust in techniques. Nevertheless, Luther did not despise the teaching of certain principles of communication that he thought were important. There are things preachers can learn regarding how to construct and deliver a sermon, and how to communicate information effectively from the pulpit.

He also said that the makeup of the human person is an important clue to preaching. God has made us in His image and has given us minds. Therefore, a sermon is addressed to the mind, but it's not just a communication of information—there is also admonition and exhortation (as noted above). There is a sense in which we are addressing people's wills and are calling them to change. We call them to act according to their understanding. In other words, we want to get to the heart, but we know that the way to the heart is through the mind. So first of all, the people must be able to understand what we're talking about. That is why Luther said it is one thing to teach in seminary, as he did at the university, and another to teach from the pulpit. He said that on Sunday mornings, he would pitch his sermons to the children in the congregation to make sure that everyone there could understand. The sermon is not to be an exercise in abstract thinking.

That which makes the deepest and most lasting impression on people is the concrete illustration. For Luther, the three most important principles of public communication were illustrate, illustrate, and illustrate. He encouraged preachers to use concrete images and narratives. He advised that, when preaching on abstract doctrine, the pastor find a narrative in Scripture that communicates that truth so as to communicate the abstract through the concrete.

In fact, that was how Jesus preached. Somebody came to Him and wanted to debate what it meant to love one's neighbor as much as oneself. "But he, wanting to justify himself, said to Jesus, 'Who is my neighbor?' Then Jesus answered and said: 'A certain man went down from Jerusalem to Jericho, and fell among thieves . . .'" (Luke 10:29–30). He didn't just give an abstract, theoretical answer to the question; he told the parable of the Good Samaritan. He answered the question in concrete form by giving a real-life situation that was sure to get the point across.

Jonathan Edwards preached his famous sermon "Sinners in the Hands of an Angry God" in Enfield, Conn. He read the sermon from a manuscript in a monotone voice. However, he employed concrete and even graphic images. For instance, Edwards said, "God . . . holds you over the pit of hell, much as one holds a spider, or some loathsome insect, over the fire."[6] Later he said, "The bow of God's wrath is bent, and the arrow made ready on the string."[7] He also declared, "You hang by a slender thread, with the flames of divine wrath flashing about it."[8] Edwards understood that the more graphic the image, the more people were likely to hear it and to remember it.

Luther said the same thing. He was not substituting technique for substance, but saying that the substance of the Word of God must be communicated in simple, graphic, straightforward, illustrative ways to the people of God. That was the whole of the matter for Luther—the minister is to be a bearer of the Word of God—nothing less, nothing more. In this way the preacher teaches the people of God.

Endnotes

---

1   Roland H. Bainton, *Here I Stand: A Life of Martin Luther* (Nashville: Abingdon, 1950), 144. Bainton notes that the words "Here I stand, I cannot do otherwise were not recorded on the spot, but appeared in the earliest printed version of Luther's statement.

2   Ewald M. Plass, *What Luther Says* (St. Louis: Concordia, 1959).

3   All Scripture quotations in this chapter are from the New King James Version.

4   Martin Luther, The Bondage of the Will (Grand Rapids: Fleming H. Revell, 1957), 67.

5   Ibid.

6   Jonathan Edwards, *A Jonathan Edwards Reader*, ed. John E. Smith, Harry S. Stout, Kenneth P. Minkema (New Haven, Conn.: Yale University Press, 2003), 97.

7   Ibid.

8   Ibid., 98.

Chapter 6

■ ■ ■

PREACHING TO THE MIND

R. C. Sproul Jr.

*W*e are all m-ad men. We are not, necessarily anyway, caught up in mental madness. Neither, I trust, are we all angry. Instead, I am suggesting that modern Americans are, by virtue of being modern Americans, given to seeing the world through advertising-colored glasses.

If, as Ken Myers so well argues in his delightful book *All God's Children and Blue Suede Shoes: The Christian and Pop Culture*, television is the dominant medium of the culture and rock-and-roll music is the dominant idiom, Madison Avenue is our dominant address. In a postmodern world, discourse does not exist for the sake of discovering truth. We do not speak to one another so that we might together discern what is so. After all, in this mindset, there is no truth to discover. Discourse in our age is designed, even as it was during the reign of the sophists in ancient Greece, to win. Language exists not to get the other guy to embrace truth, but to get him to buy what I'm selling, even when I believe it's not worth buying. According to this mindset, both ancient and postmodern, all language is a thinly veiled power play, and if we are wise, we will play wisely with words to get what we want.

When you scratch beneath the surface of the teachings of church-growth gurus, you find m-ad men. (One could argue that one need not even scratch—some of the gurus are rather upfront about their tactics.) You find consultants who are experts in the realm of advertising, who have in turn become experts in marketing not just the church, but the Lord of the church, Jesus Himself. Their counsel with respect to preaching is that we ought to become as they are, that we too must learn to market our messages, to become m-ad men behind the pulpit. Though it is madness, too many pastors agree.

Advertising itself has changed over the years. As America slowly moved from a word-based culture to an image-based culture, its advertising slowly moved from seeking to win an argument to seeking to win a customer. In the early days of television, advertisers made their case for the superiority of their products. They compared and contrasted. They brought forth their scientific studies. They sought to prove objectively that their wares were better than Brand X. Before long, however, image overcame word, and advertising turned to a subconscious association game.

This is the approach of advertising in our day. Rather than seeking to get around the natural barriers of skepticism in order to get a hearing in the mind of the consumer, advertising now seeks to get around the barrier of the mind of the consumer in order to make a sale. Advertising seeks to make an end run around our consciousness in order to get in our wallets. Consider, for example, the nearly universal pricing structure of goods and services. If you want to buy a pizza, you are likely to be able to find one for say, $5.99. Now why would Pizzas R Us sell a pizza at that price? Wouldn't it make much more sense to offer the pizza for $6? This old saw is so old that we see right through it, but Pizzas R Us still uses it. The seller is hoping that your conscious mind will think the pizza costs $5 while your wallet will be $6 lighter.

When, in like manner, a baseball hero tells us to buy a certain kind of razor blade, we do not hear a carefully crafted argument for the precision of the blade. Instead, we are encouraged to believe that buying that blade will make us more like our hero. It's a ridiculous notion once it is out in the open—which is why it is never placed out in the open. We move blithely through our lives, having our strings pulled by advertising aimed at our subconscious minds.

As bad as it is to be duped, however, it is far worse to be guilty of duping others. This is what the gurus call us to do. They want us, in calling people to embrace Jesus Christ, who is the truth, to set aside truth in favor of psychological techniques. Their techniques are powerful enough that pastors who ought to know better buy into them.

Avoiding Carnality

What God's Word calls us to do is altogether different. There we are told that the weapons of our warfare are not carnal, but have divine power to destroy strongholds (2 Cor. 10:4).[1] It is true enough that when Paul tells us this, he at least means that our weapons are not aircraft carriers and guided missiles. We do not wage war for the kingdom of God by massing troops here and flying sorties there. But the fleshiness, or carnality, that we are called to avoid goes deeper. Paul does not merely mean that our weapons are not physical. He also means that they are not sinful. Psychological manipulation can't be packed in a suitcase. Deceptive advertising doesn't occupy space. But these are carnal weapons, and not only will they not be fruitful in the great battle, they will instead be weapons in the hand of the Serpent. Even in the hands of the well-meaning believer, these techniques are bombs exploding around us, doing damage to the soldiers of the kingdom but leaving the seed of the Serpent untouched.

We fight our temptations to carnality with wisdom, with obedience, and with the power of God's Word. Paul goes on in writing to the Corinthians, saying, "We destroy arguments and every lofty opinion raised against the knowledge of God, and take every thought captive to obey Christ" (v. 5). In this verse, notice that we have some variation of the concept of mind or thought four times (arguments, opinion, knowledge, and thought). We are engaged in a battle with the Serpent and his seed. War was declared by the Serpent through the temptation of Eve. God declared war in pronouncing judgment on the Serpent in the garden: "I will put enmity between you and the woman, and between your offspring and her offspring; he shall bruise your head, and you shall bruise his heel" (Gen. 3:15). This is the war in which we fight with non-carnal weapons. In this war, we fight indeed with our hearts. We fight with our hands and feet. But we fight with our minds, as well. We destroy arguments, we tear down strongholds, and we take thoughts captive—all in and through our minds.

This is why our minds must be equipped, strengthened, fed. If we would fight faithfully against the forces of darkness, if we would labor as we ought to make known the reign of Christ over all things, we need to think sharply. We need to have minds that are on guard against the subtle wiles of the Serpent. He, to be certain, appeals to our sinful hearts, seeking to seduce our affections. But he likewise delights to cloud our minds, to confuse us, that he might lead us astray.

We soldiers of the cross are equipped in and through the foolishness of preaching. There we tap into a power not of our own devising. There we find weapons of great strength, given to us by the Spirit of God.

Now the Serpent has his weapons arrayed against God's weapons. In our own day, for instance, he has taught evangelicals to be suspicious of what he calls "head knowledge" or "dry orthodoxy." We ought to be opposed to dryness. But who could object to orthodoxy? Are our only choices "dry orthodoxy" or "wet heresy"? But given our suspicions about "head knowledge," we too often come to the Lord's Day service looking not to be informed but to be inspired. We too often come as the children of Rousseau, father of the Romantic movement, believing that the legitimacy of any event is measured by the strength of our emotional response. But even if we escape this temptation, if we don't buy into the notion that intense emotional experience is the goal, we may well make a different mistake. We may be left with sermons that are little more than lectures, data dumps whereby the professional clergyman downloads information from his prodigious brain into the minds of the flock.

In both cases, the service of worship is upside down and backward. In both cases, those who have been called to come and worship instead worship themselves, as their emotional or intellectual needs are pandered to. In both cases, the market is driving the service. The only difference is in the tastes of the different markets, one liking emotional goodies, the other preferring intellectual goodies.

When we come with a right perspective, worship is a tremendous blessing to us, but when God calls us to worship Him, He does so ultimately for His sake rather than ours. Yes, when we forget ourselves, we do find ourselves. When we die, we live. But it all begins with dying. We gather first because He calls us. And He calls us, in a manner of speaking, as a general gathers His troops for inspection. He calls us that He might assess our condition.

In the church where I serve, it is precisely for this reason that we first hear the call to worship. This is not the pastor or worship leader gathering the people and instructing them to grab one more quick cup of coffee. This is God commanding that we appear. Next, we confess our sins. When God calls you for inspection, and you know you cannot pass, it's a good thing to tell Him so. It is wise to confess our failures up front, and so we do. Next in the order of worship we hear the assurance of pardon, a passage of Scripture wherein we are reminded that God saves sinners, that He will not despise a broken and contrite heart.

From there, continuing in a process by which God speaks to us and we speak our "amens" back to him, we move through a psalm or hymn, a confession of faith, and a time of corporate prayer. Then we come to the preaching of His Word. We as a congregation stand to hear the reading of God's Word. The pastor prays the prayer of illumination, asking that God would be pleased to change us through the preaching of His Word, that we might be remade into the image of His Son. Then, finally, the Word is preached.

In this context, God is addressing the same troops He gathered together at the start of the service. He is, in a manner of speaking, giving us our marching orders, telling us what we must do that the glory of His reign might be made known. The Word is not preached that we might have a potent emotional experience. The Word is not preached that our brains might be tickled. Instead, the Word is preached that we might be instructed, that the Great Commission itself might be fulfilled, wherein Jesus commands us, "Go therefore and make disciples of all nations, baptizing them in the name of the Father and of the Son and of the Holy Spirit, teaching them to observe all that I have commanded you" (Matt. 28:19–20a). We are, through the preaching of the Word, discipled, taught, instructed.

Preaching, therefore, though it shames me even to have to say it, must be directed toward the mind of the congregant. Preaching must bring changed hearts and changed lives, both of which are, of necessity, the fruit of changed minds. We are to bring God's Word to bear in the lives of those under our care, instructing them in righteousness, directing them, in the words of Psalm 23, in the paths of righteousness. We are changed through changing our thinking. Our thinking is changed through the power of preaching, but only when that power is rightly directed. If the power is directed to avoid our minds, the power is being exercised by the enemy.

Preaching Simply

How, then, do we actually preach to the mind? How do we, in a sensate culture, escape the perpetual temptation toward manipulation? How do we escape the burning desire to entertain? We do this, ironically, by preaching simply.

A simple sermon is not what we might at first expect. My point is not to encourage the dumbing down of sermons. The goal is not to remove all big words and all subtle concepts from our sermons so that we will arrive at sound preaching to the mind. Rather, simple preaching is marked by a simplicity of purpose.

At the Highlands Study Center, where I labor, our purpose statement reads, "The Highlands Study Center exists to help Christians live more simple, separate, and deliberate lives for the glory of God and for the building of His kingdom." The study center has been around long enough that I have a pretty good idea of how people react to this statement. No one, for instance, has a strong objection to seeing God glorified or His kingdom made known. There is nothing shocking there. It is the same with the word *deliberate*. The desire for more deliberate living isn't controversial. No branch of the church is arguing that we need more sloppy, thoughtless Christian lives. The word *separate*, frankly, frightens people. I'm sure some people are put off by this term because they think it means living monastic lives. They fear we're encouraging people to be so heavenly minded that they are no earthly good. Others, perhaps, are turned off by this notion because they actually understand what we are saying and don't like it. The call to be set apart, to be a city on a hill, to be holy, is offensive not only to the world but to that which is worldly in the church.

So *deliberate* elicits yawns. *Separate* brings out concerns. But *simple* just confuses people. They don't know what we mean. *Simple*, however, is simple. It is simply a manifestation of the wisdom of Jesus, who tells us "no one can serve two masters" (Matt. 6:24a). We want our lives not to be at one and the same time about seeking first the kingdom of God while also seeking lives of personal peace and affluence. Simplicity is having one master, the Lord Jesus Christ.

This connects with preaching in a little liturgy I have practiced over the years with my father. It has been my privilege for several decades now to be on hand when my father is speaking at sundry conferences. There we find ourselves, usually several times a year, in a room filled with several thousand people. If the event is sponsored by my father's ministry, he is there with a great load on his shoulders. He not only needs to deliver a faithful address, but he is worried to some degree about the logistics of the event, about whether the other speakers are having their needs met, and perhaps even (if I am one of those other speakers) whether they will say the right things. There we sit together, usually in the front row. Typically, someone is up on the podium introducing my father. Just as he is about to leave his seat and head to the front, my habit has been to whisper these words in his ear: "Tell the truth."

To preach simply, we begin with that simple imperative, that we tell the truth. Issues of holding the congregation's attention, which walk hand in hand with temptations to bypass the mind, begin to fade as we seek to tell the truth. Even the temptation to wow the people with our superior intellect fades away when we remember our simple calling to tell the truth. "Tell the truth" is to the preacher what "First, do no harm" is to the physician.

If the Bible is a book designed to change our minds that we might change everything else, and if our overarching concern is simply that we be faithful to the Bible (and telling the truth is nothing more or less than being faithful to the Bible), then we will tell the truth, and in so doing we will preach to the mind as we preach exegetically. We will come to the Bible and not only let it tell us its truth, but let it set our agenda. When, for instance, we preach through particular books of the Bible, we will be less likely to preach our own hobbyhorses, however biblical they might be. (This means, by the way, especially for Reformed pastors, that we have not completely gotten with this program if we find ourselves over and over again preaching exegetically only Paul's theologically meaty epistles.)

As preachers of the Word, then, we begin by receiving the Word as it is "preached" to us. We will preach to the minds of the sheep as we allow our own minds to be preached to. That means that during our preparation, we come to the text less interested in what we will be saying about the text to others the next Lord's Day and more interested in what the text is saying to us on that day. This, too, might be called "simplicity." We don't divide the text into what it says to pastors and what it says to laymen. We look instead for what it says to sinners.

Next, we preach to the mind when we practice sound and simple hermeneutics. When we come to the text with a grammatico-historical approach, treating verbs as verbs and nouns as nouns (rather than treating the whole thing as a Gnostic plaything), and when we ask first, "What was the original author seeking to say to the original audience?" then we are rightly chained to the text. We have no room here for rhetorical flourish. We have no room for dazzling complexity. We have only to ask, "What does the text say?"

Preaching the Text

A caveat, however, is in order here. Though it might be a touch subtle, there is an important distinction between preaching to the mind and preaching erudite, heavy, and intellectually challenging sermons. One of the ways we get confused on this is in missing the first part of the grammatico-historical method. That is to say, when a pastor faces the temptation to demonstrate the power of his brain, the tack he is likely to take is to forget that he is exegeting literature. With all due recognition of the technicalities and complexities of moving from ancient literature to modern ears, in the end, Paul wrote letters, David wrote Psalms, Isaiah made prophecies, and so forth. None of them gave us biological samples that belong under a microscope. If you find yourself preaching for six months on a single verse of the Bible, enthralling your audience with your mastery of the original languages, your precision of logical inference, your breadth of knowledge of the ancient Near East, you have forgotten the first thing—it's a letter, a psalm, or a prophecy. We are to preach the text as it is written.

When we preach to the mind, we remember the battle. We remember that we are at war with the Serpent and his seed. We equip our hands for war by renewing our minds. This means that the foolishness of preaching must include preaching foolishness. We are not, of course, to speak our own foolishness. We are, however, to expose the wisdom of the world for the foolishness that it is.

As we practice a grammatico-historical approach, we face two challenges. First, we want, of course, to understand the original intention of the original author to the original audience. That is, we want to come to the Bible looking through the eyes of the children of Abraham. The challenge is we are not first-century Jews. But the second challenge is that we are twenty-first-century Westerners. We do not have the mindset and culture of the original audience, while we do have the mindset and culture of our own audience.

Thus, the first strongholds that must be torn down are in our own minds. They are the unexamined presuppositions that shape our thinking and our doing. They are our failures to be deliberate. Preaching to the mind, then, targets our own errors, our own blind spots. It does so by seeking to understand the "wisdom" of the age. This does not mean that a faithful preacher must spend his time and energy immersing himself into his own culture. The point isn't that we must know who the latest pop stars are so that we can be "relevant." It may mean, however, that we are aware of the broader dangers of pop culture and how those dangers seduce God's soldiers. Preaching to the mind will clear this kind of debris from our minds so that the Word can find fertile soil in which to take root. In other words, we need to remember that in the great war between the seed of the woman and the seed of the Serpent, both sides actually fight. We are to aspire to think God's thoughts after Him, but the Serpent seeks to encourage us to think his thoughts after him.

If we would seek to preach to the mind, we also must encourage those in our hearing to receive the Word preached with their minds. The habits of their hearts will be shaped by the habits of their minds. If, strangely, they listen only to check the preacher's level of orthodoxy, if they seek only to have their intellects tickled, if they attend to preaching only that they might show forth their own erudition, it is not their minds but their egos that are not being preached to. Just as a deep and complex sermon, rather than a simple and straightforward one, can be a sign of a preacher getting in the way, a deep and complex analysis of a sermon by the adept layman can be a sign of a congregant getting in the way. Our minds always need to be exhorted to beware our propensity for ego.

This kind of problem leads not to a healthy and godly mind, but to a clogged mind. While we are indeed called to preach to the mind, we must remember as well that as a man thinks in his *heart*, so he is. The mind will not be preached to if it is still in bondage to sin, if it is not being fed by a heart made new by the Spirit of God. The mind in turn will not feed the heart if it is clogged by pride. We cannot get to the heart without going through the mind, but we can get to the mind and foolishly stop there.

Our minds ought to be staggered by the glory of the gospel of Jesus Christ. This trait is evident in perhaps the greatest preacher of the church, the apostle Paul. No one could argue that Paul, in his epistles, was simple. No Christian would ever suggest that you can check your brain at the door when reading Paul. Even Peter himself acknowledged that Paul's epistles were not always easy to understand (2 Peter 3:16). But Paul was no dry classroom teacher. His heavy theology is punctuated always with outbursts of doxology. Paul begins to expound on the atonement of Christ and breaks into song. He begins to explain the fruit of the gospel, our end, and breaks into glorious praise. Paul was a man whose mind and heart were intimately connected. The next chapter of this book looks at the call to preach to the heart. My calling has been to deal with the mind. But preaching to the mind is not something we do on the first and third Sundays of the month, while we preach to the heart on the second and fourth. These are not merely parallel obligations; they are intimately tied together. The end goal is not only that we would be transformed by the renewing of our minds, but that all that we are would be transformed. We want minds informed. We want hearts enflamed. And we want hands equipped.

In the end, we will reach our ends only when we aim not to preach to the mind or to the heart. We will rightly do both these things only when we preach the Word. It is the source of the power to change the world. It never returns void. It is the power to tear down strongholds and every lofty thing that exalts itself against the knowledge of Christ. It is the blessing that will drive us to take every thought captive. As it takes root in our hearts and minds, we will no longer be m-ad men. We will instead be remade men.

Endnotes

---

[1] All Scripture quotations in this chapter are from the English Standard Version.

Chapter 7

■ ■ ■

PREACHING TO THE HEART

Sinclair B. Ferguson

*N*o more poignant or instructive description of the work of the minister of the gospel exists than Paul's "defensive excursus"[1] in 2 Corinthians 2:14–7:4. Every Christian preacher should aim to possess a good working knowledge of this seminal part of the New Testament, in which Paul simultaneously describes and defends his service as an apostle of Jesus Christ and a minister of the new covenant. He uses this language explicitly when he affirms, "God has made us competent as ministers of a new covenant" (2 Cor. 3:6). In what follows, he takes us from the outside of his ministry to its deep internal roots:

> Therefore, since through God's mercy we have this ministry, we do not lose heart. Rather, we have renounced secret and shameful ways; we do not use deception, nor do we distort the word of God. On the contrary, by setting forth the truth plainly we commend ourselves to every man's conscience in the sight of God. And even if our gospel is veiled, it is veiled to those who are perishing. The god of this age has blinded the minds of unbelievers, so that they cannot see the light of the gospel of the glory of Christ, who is the image of God. For we do not preach ourselves, but Jesus Christ as Lord, and ourselves as your servants for Jesus' sake. For God, who said, "Let light shine out of darkness," made his light shine in our hearts to give us the light of the knowledge of the glory of God in the face of Christ.
>
> But we have this treasure in jars of clay to show that this all-surpassing power is from God and not from us. We are hard pressed on every side, but

not crushed; perplexed, but not in despair; persecuted, but not abandoned; struck down, but not destroyed. We always carry around in our body the death of Jesus, so that the life of Jesus may also be revealed in our body. For we who are alive are always being given over to death for Jesus' sake, so that His life may be revealed in our mortal body. So then, death is at work in us, but life is at work in you.

It is written, "I believed, therefore I have spoken." With that same spirit of faith we also believe and therefore speak, because we know that the one who raised the Lord Jesus from the dead will also raise us with Jesus and present us with you in his presence. All this is for your benefit, so that the grace that is reaching more and more people may cause thanksgiving to overflow to the glory of God.

Therefore we do not lose heart. Though outwardly we are wasting away, yet inwardly we are being renewed day by day. For our light and momentary troubles are achieving for us an eternal glory that far outweighs them all. So we fix our eyes not on what is seen, but what is unseen. For what is seen is temporary, but what is unseen is eternal. (2 Cor. 4:1–18)[2]

The title of this chapter is "Preaching to the Heart." All truly biblical preaching is preaching to the heart. Therefore, it is important that we have a clear idea of what "preaching to the heart" means.

The Heart

In Scripture, the word *heart* only rarely denotes the physical organ. It characteristically refers to the central core of the individual's being and personality: the deep-seated element of a person that provides both the energy and the drive for all of the faculties (e.g., Deut. 4:9; Matt. 12:34). It denotes the governing center of life.

Interestingly, of the 858 occurrences of the Hebrew terms that are translated as "heart," *leb* and *lebab*, almost all have reference to human beings (in distinction from either God or other creatures). Indeed, "heart" is the Old Testament's major anthropological term.[3]

Modern Westerners tend to think of the heart as the center of a person's emotional life (hence its use as the symbol of romantic rather than volitional love). But the Hebrew conceptualization placed the emotional center lower in the anatomy and located the intellectual energy center of a person in the heart. Hence, the word *heart* is frequently used as a synonym for the mind, the will, and the conscience, as well as (on occasion) for the affections. It refers to the fundamental bent or characteristic of an individual's life.

In this sense, when we think about speaking or preaching to the heart, we do not have in view directly addressing the emotions as such. In any event, as Jonathan Edwards argued with such force, the mind cannot be so easily bypassed. Rather, we are thinking of preaching that influences the very core and center of an individual's being, making an impact on the whole person, including the emotions, but doing so primarily by instructing and appealing to the mind. Such a focus is of paramount importance for preachers because the transformation and the renewal of the heart is what is chiefly in view in their proclamation of the gospel (cf. Rom. 12:1–2).

This, in fact, is already implied in Paul's description of himself and his companions as "competent ministers of a new covenant" (2 Cor. 3:6). Built into the foundation of the new covenant is the promise of a transformed heart: "I will sprinkle clean water on you, and you will be clean. I will cleanse you from all your impurities and from all your idols. I will give you a new heart. . . . I will remove from you your heart of stone and give you a heart of flesh" (Ezek. 36:25–26).

No matter what circumstances under which we preach the Word of God, no matter to whom we are speaking, insofar as we too are called to be "competent ministers of the new covenant," our preaching must always have the heart in view.

Threefold Openness

Paul speaks more fully here about his own preaching ministry than anywhere else in the New Testament. One of the key notes he strikes is that his preaching to the heart was marked by a threefold openness:

1. It involved an openness of Paul's being, a transparency before God. "What we are," he says, "is plain to God" (2 Cor. 5:11).

2. It also implied an opening out of the love that filled his heart toward the people to whom he was ministering. "We have . . . opened wide our hearts to you" (2 Cor. 6:11).

3. Within that twofold context—his own heart opened vertically toward God and horizontally toward those to whom he was seeking to minister—Paul's preaching to the heart was also characterized by a disclosing (an opening up) of the truth. He expresses this in an illuminating way when he describes it as "setting forth the truth plainly" (2 Cor. 4:2), what the King James Version describes more graphically as "the manifestation of the truth."

Thus, just as he is an open book in the sight of God, similarly the preacher lays open the integrity of his life to the consciences and hearts of his hearers as though he were a letter to be read by them (cf. 2 Cor. 3:2). But these characteristics are never isolated from the way in which we handle the Scriptures, opening up and laying bare their message in both exposition and application. The Corinthians had seen these hallmarks in Paul's ministry. They were a large part of the explanation for his ministry's power and fruit. They are no less essential to the minister of the gospel today, if he is to preach with similar effect on the hearts of his hearers.

Preaching to the heart, then, is not merely a matter of technique or homiletic style. These things have their proper place and relevance. But the more fundamental, indeed, the more essential thing for the preacher is surely the fact that something has happened in his own heart; it has been laid bare before God by His Word. He, in turn, lays his heart bare before those to whom he ministers. And within that context, the goal he has in view is so to lay bare the truth of the Word of God that the hearts of those who hear are opened vertically to God and horizontally to one another.

Paul had reflected on this impact of God's Word in 1 Corinthians 14, in the context of his discussion of tongues and prophecy in the Corinthian church. Prophetic utterance always possesses an element of speaking "to the heart" (Isa. 40:2).[4] Through such preaching, even someone who comes in from the outside finds that "the secrets of his heart will be laid bare. So he will fall down and worship God, exclaiming 'God is really among you'" (1 Cor. 14:24–25).

In the last analysis, this is what preaching to the heart is intended to produce: inner prostration of the hearts of our listeners through a consciousness of the presence and the glory of God. This result distinguishes authentic biblical preaching from any cheap substitute; it marks the difference between preaching *about* the Word of God and preaching *the* Word of God.

The presence of this threefold openness, then, is most desirable in preaching. When there is the exposition of the Scriptures, an enlarging and opening of the preacher's heart, and the exposing of the hearts of the hearers, then the majesty of the Word of God *written* will be self-evident and the presence of the Word of God *Incarnate* will stand forth in all His glory.

Man Small, God Great

There is a widespread need for this kind of preaching. We have an equal need as preachers to catch the vision for it in an overly pragmatic and programmatic society that believes it is possible to live the Christian life without either the exposing of our own hearts or the accompanying prostration of ourselves before the majesty of God on high.

It is just here that one notices a striking contrast between the biblical exposition one finds in the steady preaching of John Calvin in the sixteenth century and preaching in our own day. It is clearly signaled by the words with which he ended virtually every one of his thousands of sermons: "And now let us bow down before the majesty of our gracious God. . . ." Reformed biblical exposition elevates God and abases man. By contrast, much modern preaching seems to have the goal of making man feel great, even if God Himself has to bow down.

So a leading characteristic of preaching to the heart will be the humbling, indeed, the prostration of hearts before the majesty of God on high. This is simultaneously the true ecstasy of the Christian, and therein lies the paradox of grace: the way down is always the way up.

But if, through the preaching of the gospel, we want to see people prostrated with mingled awe and joy before God, the essential prerequisite is that we ourselves be prostrated before him. John Owen's words still ring true even after three and a half centuries: "a man preacheth that sermon only well unto others which preacheth itself in his own soul. . . . If the word do not dwell with power *in* us, it will not pass with power *from* us."[5]

Preaching to the heart—through whatever personality, in whatever style—will always exhibit the following five characteristics:

1. *A right use of the Bible.* Preaching to the heart is undergirded by our familiarity with the use of sacred Scripture. According to 2 Timothy 3:16, all Scripture is useful (*ophelimos*) for certain practical functions: for teaching, rebuking, correcting, and training in righteousness, so that the man of God may be thoroughly equipped for every good work.

If it were not for the fact that a chapter division appears in our Bibles at this point (giving the impression that Paul is now changing gears in his charge to Timothy), we would not so easily miss the point implicit in what he goes on to say. In 2 Timothy 4:1–2, Paul takes up these same uses of Scripture (teaching, rebuking, correcting, encouraging in godly living) and applies them. In effect, he says to Timothy, "Use the God-breathed Scriptures this way in your ministry!"

Those who love the richer, older theology of the Reformation and Puritan eras, and of Jonathan Edwards and Thomas Boston, may be tempted to look askance at the modern professor of preaching as he hands out copies of his "preaching grid" to the incoming class of freshmen taking Homiletics 101. But the fact is that here we find Paul handing out the last copy of his own "preaching grid" to Timothy! This is by no means the only preaching grid to be found, either in Scripture or in the Reformed tradition,[6] but it certainly is a grid that ought to be built into our basic approach to preaching.

Thus informed, we come to see that preaching to the heart will give expression to four things: instruction in the truth, conviction of the conscience, restoration and transformation of life,[7] and equipping for service.[8] Let us not think that we have gained so much maturity in Christian living and service that we can bypass the fundamental structures that the apostles give us to help us practically in these areas.

Preaching, therefore, involves teaching—imparting doctrine in order to renew and transform the mind. It implies the inevitable rebuke of sin, and brings with it the healing of divine correction. The language of "correction" (*epanorthosis*) is used in the Septuagint for the rebuilding of a city or the repair of a sanctuary.[9] Outside of biblical Greek, it is used in the medical textbooks of the ancient world for the setting of broken limbs. It is a word that belongs to the world of reconstruction, remedy, healing, and restoration.

This brings us to another characteristic of the apostle Paul: a masterful balance between the negation of sin and the edification of the Christian believer, "so that the man of God may be thoroughly equipped for every good work." If we are going to preach to the heart, then our preaching will always (admittedly in different kinds of balance) be characterized by these four marks of authenticity.

But such preaching must first be directed to the mind. When we preach to the heart, we are not engaged in rebuking the conscience or cleansing the emotions directly. Rather, preaching to the heart addresses the understanding first, in order to instruct it; but in doing so it also reaches through the mind to inform, rebuke, and cleanse the conscience. It then touches the will in order to reform and transform life and equip the saints for the work of ministry (Eph. 4:12).

When we preach to the heart, the mind is not so much the terminus of our preaching, but the channel through which we appeal to the whole person, leading to the transformation of the whole life.

2. *Nourishment of the whole person.* There is an important balance to be pursued here—the balance of ministering to the understanding, affections, and will. It is very easy to lose sight of this. Its significance may perhaps best be underlined by means of a personal illustration.

Many years ago, I had the privilege of preaching on a few occasions to a particular congregation. During this period (and with no connection between these events!), the pastor of the church received and accepted a call to serve elsewhere. Friends whom I made during these occasional visits confided in me some time after the departure of their pastor (to whom they were extremely loyal): "As we have sought to assess the impact of these last years of ministry on our lives, we have come to this conclusion: while we were thoroughly well-instructed, we were poorly nourished."

There is a difference between a well-instructed congregation and a well-nourished one. It is possible to instruct, yet fail to nourish those to whom we preach. It is possible to address the mind, but to do so with little concern to see the conscience, the heart, and the affections reached and cleansed, the will redirected, and the whole person transformed through a renewed mind. By contrast, in the picture of preaching first painted for Timothy, Paul is teaching us how to preach to the heart in a way that will nourish the whole person.

One of the characteristics of such preaching is pathos, the stimulation in us of a sense of sadness, even brokenheartedness. Pathos is not mere emotion for its own sake, certainly not the kind of emotionalism that tends to descend into an insincere, over-the-top expressiveness. In preaching, it is, rather, the communication and evoking through our words of the responsive "mood" appropriate to sinners listening to the gospel being preached. In this way, our hearers become aware of the power of the truths we are preaching about human sin, divine grace, and glory.

The great Welsh preacher Dr. D. Martyn Lloyd-Jones once made a fascinating and illuminating (to me, at least) self-critical comment on what he felt had been a weaknesses of his own preaching ministry. He thought it had lacked in at least one particular aspect—pathos.

Christians of an earlier time sometimes spoke of sermons as "pathetic." We, of course, would not cross the street to hear preaching if it was "pathetic" in the modern sense of the word. But our forefathers meant something quite different by this expression, namely, preaching that leaves its hearers with melted hearts. The preaching that does this comes from a similarly broken and melted heart that already has placed itself under this four-fold applicatory grid of Scripture: the preaching heart has been instructed by the truth of Scripture; the conscience rebuked by the holiness of Scripture; and the spirit nourished by the correction, healing, and restorative power of Scripture, so that the man of God, the preacher, is equipped to relate God's Word from his own heart to our hearts.

3. *An understanding of the condition of the hearers.* Preaching to the heart always reflects an awareness of the actual condition of our hearers. In one form or another, most preaching books underscore this point. The preacher emerges from the world of the biblical text to speak in the name of Christ to the world of his hearers.

One of the hidden snares in systematic biblical preaching is that we may become so taken up with the task of studying and explaining the text that we forget the actual poverty and falsehood it addresses. One distinctively Reformed manifestation of this is that our love for the works of the past (coupled with their ready availability today)—our discovery, for example, of the depth of Puritan preaching by comparison with contemporary preaching—may suck us into the very language and speech patterns of a past era, thus making us sound inauthentic to our own generation.

By contrast, preaching to the heart will not be encrusted with layers of ill-digested materials from the past, however relevant these were in their own day. Those preaching helps must rather be thoroughly digested, made our own, and applied to people today in today's language. That is what it means to bring the truth to bear upon men, women, boys, and girls in such a way that it opens up and penetrates their hearts.

In this sense, biblical exposition must speak to the people sitting today in the pews, not to those who sat in them hundreds of years ago. This, in fact, is one of the cardinal principles expounded by William Perkins in his great work *The Arte of Prophecying* (sic), the original Puritan manual on preaching. Perkins argues that we have to understand the *soul-condition* of those to whom we preach, and address them in an appropriate and relevant way.

We always preach to people in a variety of spiritual conditions. Perkins realized that if he was going to touch people with the truth of the gospel, then he must—always in a manner consistent with the gospel—explain and apply his text. Only then would it serve as a sharp instrument that the Holy Spirit, the Divine Surgeon, might use to cut open the hearts of the people and bring healing to their diseased spirits. In that sense, the way we explain the Scriptures can never be abstracted from the characteristics, personality, and maturity level of those to whom we preach.

Perkins' own grid is inherently interesting and valuable, if one employs it in a way that makes it genuinely one's own. He suggests that preaching should be shaped to six categories of hearers:

• Non-Christians who know nothing about the gospel and have unteachable spirits.

• Non-Christians who know nothing about the gospel but who are teachable.

• Those who know what the gospel is but who have never been humbled to see their need of a Savior.

• Those who have been humbled, some of whom are in the early stages of seeing their need, and others who see that they need salvation, not merely improvement, and are now convinced that only Christ can save them.

• Genuine believers who need to be taught.

• Backsliders, either because of a failure to understand the gospel clearly or a failure to live consistently with it.

As Perkins acknowledged, most preachers will serve mixed congregations. In other words, they will generally preach simultaneously to all six types of hearers.[10]

But we do not need to appeal to the Puritans for the authority to operate with this type of "preaching grid"; our Lord Jesus did so Himself. On at least one

occasion, He divided His hearers into four categories and likened them to different kinds of soil distinguished by their receptivity to the cultivation of seed: the
hard-packed soil of the pathway, the rocky soil, the weed-infested soil, and the
good soil (Mark 4:1–20).

It would make a fascinating academic study of the ministry of Jesus to take this
parable of the sower, the seed, and the soils as a lens through which to examine,
categorize, and analyze His preaching. For preachers, too, it is a fruitful exercise to
consider the ways in which He applied His message to the four spiritual conditions
to which He saw Himself speaking.

Is it because expository preaching is such a demanding activity, and we are so
consumed by its demands, that some of us pay so little attention (or at least too
little attention) to the spiritual condition of those to whom we are preaching? If so,
we need to reconsider our approach.

If it is important that we know the condition of the hearts of our hearers, the
best place to begin is, of course, with our own hearts. If we apply the Word there,
we soon will learn to be like surgical attendants: our exposition of the text will
become like sterilized knives, perfectly tooled, that we hand to the Spirit for the
precise spiritual surgery that our people need.

A further feature that characterized our Lord Jesus' preaching was that the
common people heard Him gladly (Mark 12:37). We ought not to dismiss this
with the cheap comment that they soon changed their tune. They immediately and
instinctively recognized the difference between the book learning and authority-
citing style of the scribes and the applied biblical wisdom and heart knowledge
displayed in Jesus' preaching. The scribes and teachers of the law spoke about the
Bible in a manner removed from daily experience. Jesus, in stark contrast, seemed
to speak from inside the Bible in a way that addressed their hearts.

Sadly, some of our preaching carries with it the atmosphere of being "about
the Bible" rather than conveying a sense that here the Bible is speaking, and indeed
God Himself is speaking. This will be changed only when we come to Scripture
in the spirit of the Servant of the Lord: "The Sovereign LORD has given me an
instructed tongue, to know the word that sustains the weary. He wakens me morning by morning, wakens my ear to listen like one being taught. The Sovereign
LORD has opened my ears, and I have not been rebellious; I have not drawn back"
(Isa. 50:4–5).

4. *The use of the imagination.* Preaching to the heart is aided by our recognition of the true nature of our task. The great question is: How, through the work of the Spirit, can I best get the Word of God into the hearts of the people?

Those who do this with the greatest fruitfulness and success are marked by many gifts and characteristics, often very diverse. But one thing all of them seem to have in common is imagination—an imaginative creativity that bridges the distance between the truth of the Word of God and the lives of those to whom they speak.

In some preachers, this is most evident in the imaginative power of their illustrations. George Whitefield's use of illustrations was sometimes so vivid that people thought they were actually caught up in the events he was describing, confusing what they were hearing with reality. By contrast, the congregation of St. Peter's Church in Geneva listened to John Calvin preach an average of five 40-minute sermons a week during the course of his lengthy ministry, but with virtually no stories or illustrations of that kind.

Like most of us, Calvin did not possess Whitfield's imaginative power (or his magical voice). Nevertheless, his sermons *lived* and had the power to stir young men to be willing to suffer martyrdom for Christ, for Calvin had an ability to use language with such imaginative power that his preaching bridged the gap between life in ancient Judah and Israel and life in sixteenth-century Geneva, Switzerland. He expressed and applied the truth in a way that was saturated in the language of the daily life of his hearers, bringing the Word of God right into the nitty-gritty practicalities of their experience.

Similarly, Richard Baxter preached in such a way that his sermons so connected with life in seventeenth-century Kidderminster, England, that the truth he spoke exploded during the week like time bombs planted in his congregation's memories.

The Spirit is able to use different sets of imaginative skills employed in different contexts but producing similar effects. But clearly the ability to imagine the Word being taken from the Scriptures and implanted into the minds of the hearers is common to all lively exposition.

Scripture itself employs different metaphors to help us grasp how important it is to "see ourselves into" the hearts and situations of those to whom we preach. Here are some drawn simply at random: the preacher is a sower of seed; a teacher of students; a father of children; a mother giving birth; a nurse feeding infants;

a shepherd caring for his flock; a soldier engaging in warfare; and a builder constructing the temple of God.

We need only to think of ourselves in terms of these metaphors to see what is involved in bringing the Word of God to bear upon the hearts and consciences of those to whom we are preaching. What does a farmer do? He plows the ground and sows the seed, then prayerfully waits for the fruition of his work. What does a builder do? He clears a building site and erects the building. What does a shepherd do? He feeds and protects his flock. How, then, can I get the seed into this soil? How can I clear the site and chisel this stone into shape? How can I prepare this meal for these people?

In these different ways, we come to recognize what it means to be a preacher. Our own imagination is fired and we begin to learn how to preach to the heart.

5. *Grace in Christ.* The fifth key to fruitful preaching to the heart is the preacher's own grasp of the principle and the reality of grace. This needs to be set within the multi-faceted context of a growing familiarity with the uses of sacred Scripture, an awareness of the actual condition of our hearers, and a conscious recognition of the preacher's task. But always the melody line of preaching to the heart lies in our own grasp of the principle of grace. That is what makes preaching "sing," and it applies to two aspects of our preaching.

First, it applies to the *content* of our preaching. Only the preaching of grace can open the sinful heart. Unaided law, imperatives without indicatives, cannot pry open locked hearts. It is grace, and—yes—the preaching of the law in the context of grace, expounding the grace of law, that brings conviction of sin. This is the very point John Newton so famously made in the best-known of his Olney Hymns, "Amazing Grace!":

> *'Twas grace that taught my heart to fear,*
> *And grace my fears relieved.*

Paul stressed this to the Corinthians. The heart and soul of his ministry was this commitment: "I resolved to know nothing while I was with you except Jesus Christ and him crucified" (1 Cor. 2:2). Through such preaching, there was a *phanerosis*, a manifestation ("setting forth," 2 Cor. 4:2) of the truth, a making known of what Paul calls "the light of the gospel of the glory of Christ, who is the image of God" (2 Cor. 4:4). For when "Jesus Christ as Lord" is thus manifested in preaching, God again makes "his light shine in our hearts to give us the light of the knowledge of the glory of God in the face of Christ" (2 Cor. 4:6).

A caveat is in order here, which is particularly relevant to a time like our own when the ancient patristic and Reformation style of consecutive exposition (the *lectio continua* method) has undergone something of a revival. We must never make the mistake of thinking that any system of consecutive exposition of Scripture absolutely guarantees the preaching of Christ. It is possible to naively assume that because we are preaching systematically through books of the Bible, we are inevitably preaching Christ and Him crucified. That ought to be the case, but it is not necessarily so. Sadly, one may preach in a consecutive way through the Bible without truly preaching Christ-centered sermons.

In addition, we may major on the theme of grace in a way that is disconnected from Christ Himself, treating it as a commodity and losing sight of the fact that it can be found only through a person.

There is a center to the Bible and its message of grace. It is found in Jesus Christ crucified and resurrected. Grace, therefore, must be preached in a way that is centered and focused on Jesus Christ Himself. We must never offer the benefits of the gospel without the Benefactor Himself. For many preachers, however, it is much easier to deal with the pragmatic things, to answer "how to" questions, and even to expose and denounce sin than it is to give an adequate explanation of the source of the forgiveness, acceptance, and power we need.

It is a disheartening fact that evangelical Christians, who write vast numbers of Christian books, preach abundant sermons, sponsor numerous conferences and seminars, and broadcast myriad TV and radio programs actually write few books, preach few sermons, sponsor few conferences or seminars, and devote few programs to the theme of Jesus Christ and Him crucified. We give our best and most creative energies to teaching God's people almost everything except the person and work of our Lord and Savior. This should cause us considerable alarm, for there is reason to fear that our failure here has reached epidemic proportions.

We need to return to a true preaching to the heart, rooted in the principle of grace and focused on the person of the Lord Jesus Christ. Then people will not say about our ministry merely, "He was an expository preacher," or "That was practical," or even "He cut open our consciences." Instead, they will say: "He preached

Christ to me, and his preaching was directed to my conscience. It was evident that he gave the best of his intellectual skills and the warmth of his compassion to thinking about, living for, and proclaiming his beloved Savior, Jesus Christ." This is what will reach the heart! And when you have experienced such preaching, or seen its fruit, you will know what true preaching is. And you will agree that its fruit lasts for all eternity.

Second, this principle of grace in Christ applies to the *manner* of our preaching.

Even today, 165 years after his early death, when we read the memoirs or the sermons of someone like Robert Murray McCheyne, we can still feel the power that must have gripped people as his preaching reached into their hearts. On the morning of McCheyne's death, a letter of gratitude for what turned out to be the last sermon he ever preached reached him. It was left unopened on his desk, and he never read the words of a grateful listener who commented, "It was not so much what you said *as your manner of your speaking*."[11] This is a major key to reaching the heart in preaching. For while preaching involves bringing the world of the Bible to bear upon the world of our contemporaries, it also involves bringing the message-in-words of the Scriptures through the message-in-manner of the preacher.

There needs to be a marriage between the message and the manner; therein lies the heart of the mystery of preaching. As our hearts are opened wide to the grace of God in the gospel, and simultaneously opened wide to our hearers, the power of the gospel is set on display (see 2 Cor. 6:11). Paul expresses this memorably in 2 Corinthians 4:5: "We do not preach ourselves, but Jesus Christ as Lord." But there is a corollary to this: "We ourselves are your bondslaves for Jesus' sake." The evidence that I preach Jesus Christ as Lord is found not so much in my declarations as it is in the manifestation of the lordship of Christ in my life and preaching— when I, His bondslave, am willing to be and actually become in my preaching the bondslave of others for Jesus' sake.

In the last analysis, preaching to the heart is preaching Christ in a way that reminds people of Christ, but also manifests Christ to them, and draws them to Him. If, among other things, preaching is (as Phillips Brooks' famous description claims) "the bringing of truth through personality,"[12] then the personalities of the preachers of the cross must be marked by the cross. So we are called to be cruciformed (shaped by the cross), Christophers (bearing the Christ of the cross), and Christplacarders (setting Christ and Him crucified on display, cf. Gal. 3:1) in our preaching as we "try to persuade men" (2 Cor. 5:11).

Perhaps such preaching of Christ is less common than we assume. If so, it is because we do not yet know Him nearly well enough.

Let us then resolve, above all other ambitions, to know Him, the power of His resurrection, and the fellowship of His sufferings (Phil. 3:10). Let us also be determined to know nothing but Jesus Christ and Him crucified (1 Cor. 2:2), so that, as we preach to the heart, God Himself will speak to His people heart to heart.

Endnotes

[1] The expression is that of Paul Barnett, *The Second Epistle to the Corinthians* (Grand Rapids: Eerdmans, 1997), 210.

[2] All Scripture quotations in this chapter are from the New International Version.

[3] H. W. Wolff, *Anthropology of the Old Testament*, trans. M. Kohl (London: SCM Press, 1974), 40–55.

[4] "Speak tenderly" (Isa. 40:2, NIV) is, literally, "speak to (or, upon) the heart" (cf. Gen. 34:3; Hosea 2:14).

[5] John Owen, *The True Nature of a Gospel Church*, in *The Works of John Owen*, ed. W. H. Goold (Edinburgh, 1853), 16:76. This has been reprinted by the Banner of Truth Trust.

[6] I am thinking here of our Lord's "grid" in the parable of the sower and the soils (Mark 4:1–20), and of the seminal work of the early English Puritan William Perkins, *The Arte of Prophecying* (Latin 1592, English 1606).

[7] *Epanorthosis*; "correction" here carries the positive connotation of "restoration."

[8] *Exertismenos*; the same root *(artizo)* is used of the goal of the ministry of the Word in Ephesians 4:12 and of the disciples washing, mending, and preparing their nets in Mark 1:19.

[9] See Çeslas Spicq, *Theological Lexicon of the New Testament*, trans. and ed. James D. Ernest (Peabody, Mass.: Hendrickson, 1994), 2:30–31.

[10] Perkins, *The Arte of Prophecying*, in *The Works of William Perkins* (London, 1617), 2:665–668. For an edited and modernized version, see *The Art of Prophesying*, ed. S. B. Ferguson (Edinburgh: Banner of Truth Trust, 1996), 56–63.

[11] Alexander Smellie, *Robert Murray McCheyne* (London: National Council of Free Evangelical Churches, 1913), 203–204.

[12] Phillips Brooks, *Lectures on Preaching* (London, n.d., first published in London in 1877), 5.

Chapter 8

■ ■ ■

PREACHING WITH AUTHORITY

Don Kistler

*J*esus must have been an amazing preacher, because Scripture tells us that when He preached people were amazed. But what was the source of their amazement? He taught as one who had authority, *not* like the scribes and Pharisees (Matt. 7:28–29).

It is to be feared that we have far too many scribes and Pharisees in pulpits today. They do not preach with authority and the people are not amazed—amused, perhaps, but not amazed. Nowadays, preachers make suggestions; they do not preach with authority. We hear things like, "I think that what God is suggesting here is. . . ." But God doesn't make suggestions, He gives commands. He did not give us the Ten Suggestions. One comedian has said that in his church they have six commandments and four "do-the-best-you-can's." That may be funny, but it is not biblical.

Jesus preached with authority. Why? Because He had authority. Likewise, the preachers of old preached with authority. They preached, "Thus saith the Lord." We have lost that today, I'm afraid. Our preaching reflects it and the lives of our people reflect it. They live as if the pastor has no authority, as if the elders have no authority, and, even more appalling, as if the Word of God itself has no authority. Old Testament Israel once fell into such ignorance of divine authority that "everyone did what was right in his own eyes" (Judg. 21:25b).[1] Something similar is true today: every man thinks what is right in his own mind, regardless of what Scripture or sound exegesis may say.

Paul's View of Pulpit Authority

Paul was a firm believer in the authority of the pulpit. In his letter to Titus, he writes: "These things speak and exhort and reprove with all authority. Let no one disregard you" (2:15). The things Titus was to speak about with authority were things most preachers today wouldn't dream of addressing, such as women subjecting themselves to their husbands. Titus was not to suggest, cajole, entice, or stroke his people. He was to convince the people of the truth of what he was saying. All these admonitions from Paul are in the command mode. In fact, the word translated as "authority" also can be rendered "command." Paul wanted Titus to preach in the command mode. As Richard Baxter puts it, Titus was to "screw the truth into [men's] minds."[2]

Paul gave a similar injunction to Timothy: "I solemnly charge you in the presence of God and of Christ Jesus, who is to judge the living and the dead, and by His appearing and His kingdom: preach the word; be ready in season and out of season" (2 Tim. 4:1–2a). How was Timothy to preach? "Reprove, rebuke, exhort, with great patience and instruction" (v. 2b). The Greek word translated as "instruction" here is *didache*, which means "teaching." Timothy was to teach the people patiently, but above all, he was called to teach them something!

In Jeremiah 3:15, God defined a preacher's call: "I will give you shepherds after My own heart." What a calling! But what does it mean to be a pastor after God's own heart? What would grant a man such a designation? A great bedside manner? Excellent people skills? Frequent visitation in the homes of his people? No, it is none of those things. God goes on to say, "I will give you shepherds after My own heart, who will feed you on knowledge and understanding." That's what makes a man a pastor after God's own heart. He feeds God's people with knowledge and understanding. In other words, he gives them doctrine and application.

Was that not also the call Christ gave to Peter? "Feed My sheep," Jesus said (John 21:17b, NKJV).

There was an article some years ago in the now-defunct *National and International Religion Report* about the moving of the Spirit of God among the Navajo Indians in the United States. One of their spokesmen said that if someone tried to preach for only twenty minutes, he would be thrown out. "They don't come to leave empty," he said.

Likewise, I have a dear friend who often supplies the pulpit in an African American church in Pittsburgh. His first time there was an eye-opener for him. He was introduced to speak after an hour and forty minutes. He asked his host how long he had to preach. The response was, "Till you're done, brother; we didn't come here to leave!"

Paul has already anticipated objections. In 2 Timothy 4:3–4, he writes, "For the time will come when they will not endure sound doctrine; but wanting to have their ears tickled, they will accumulate for themselves teachers in accordance with their own desires; and will turn away their ears from the truth, and will turn aside to myths." A pastor might say: "That's the problem. My people won't take that from me. There would be a mutiny if I preached like that!"

But what does Paul say? "But you, be sober in all things, endure hardship, do the work of an evangelist, fulfill your ministry." Do you see what he is saying? Your calling doesn't change when the group dynamics of your congregation change. You don't change your message just because they don't like it. You are preaching to please the Lord, not your people! Your calling is from Him; it is His approval that matters. It is He who will declare (or will not declare), "Well done, thou good and faithful servant" (Matt. 25:21a, KJV).

We can preach with authority because Christ has given us authority. Did He not say: "All authority has been given to Me in heaven and on earth. Go therefore and make disciples of all the nations . . . teaching them to observe all that I commanded you" (Matt. 28:18b–20a)? It wasn't "teaching them to observe all that I have *suggested* to you," but "all that I have *commanded* you"!

Of course, ministers must remember that any authority they have is a granted or delegated authority. Christ, who is the Author, has the authority. Ministers have no inherent authority; it is all derived. So in that sense, a minister cannot imitate His authority, but he can imitate Christ's zeal and boldness. It was in this regard that Paul solicited prayer from the Ephesians (Eph. 6:19).

God Speaking to Men

Romans 10 gives us a picture of Paul's pastoral heart. He states that his heart's desire for the people is their salvation. Any pastor who feels differently is not a faithful minister of Jesus Christ. I remember when the presbytery committee on evangelism came to the church I was pastoring and asked what we were doing evangelistically. My response was that we were trying to lead some of our members to salvation! I wasn't kidding; my heart's desire for many in my congregation was that they would be saved.

Then Paul begins to reveal the process by which God ordinarily is pleased to save souls. In verse 13, he declares that whoever shall call upon the name of the Lord shall be saved. But he then raises a series of questions: "How then shall they call upon Him in whom they have not believed? And how shall they believe in Him whom they have not heard. And how shall they hear without a preacher? And how shall they preach unless they are sent?" (vv. 14–15a).

Notice that Paul does not ask how they shall hear *about* Christ, but how they shall hear *Him* without a preacher! Do you see what Paul is saying here? When the faithful minister is properly exegeting the Word of God, it is God Himself who is speaking to His people, drawing them to Himself! Failure to hear the faithful minister is a failure to hear God Himself!

Isn't that exactly what Jesus told His disciples? He said, "The one who listens to you listens to Me, and the one who rejects you rejects Me" (Luke 10:16a). We must not to let anyone disregard us, because that would mean we were letting them disregard Christ. "How shall they hear Christ without a preacher?" That is the question! A faithful minister is the mouthpiece of God!

Preachers are one of the love gifts of the ascended Christ to His body, the church. We should never let anyone denigrate the sacred calling of a pastor to stand in his pulpit and faithfully exegete the inspired Word of God to the people of God, thereby carrying out his ministry to be the mouthpiece of God.

Pastors must deliver God's Word to His people in such a manner that the majesty and authority of it is preserved. Have you ever noticed that whenever the Scriptures are read in the biblical accounts, all the people stand up out of reverence? Not so with us. We sit! Why is that? Why do we not follow this tradition of standing up out of reverence for God's Word?

And why do preachers often act as if what they are saying is simply their opinion? Preachers are not called to give their opinions; they are supposed to give the people the very mind of God. The people love it when no one is in charge. They love it when the pastor is on the same level as they are. They love it when they share authority as peers. However, they *don't* love it when pastors preach. At any other time in a preacher's life, he is on the same level as his people; but when he mounts the pulpit, he becomes something else entirely—a voice of authority.

When Jesus preached, He didn't wait for someone to validate His message or authority. He would say "Truly I say to you . . ." at the beginning of His message, not at the end. What He said wasn't open for debate.

Preaching for Conviction and Change

Too often preachers give their people the impression that all they need to do is think about what has been said. How many times have you heard it said, "Well, pastor, you've given me a lot to think about"? Thinking and reflecting are good things, but action is needed in the end. God never gave us His Word to simply think about, but to obey. Others think the sermon is merely to be a topic for conversation. Thomas Watson, in a sermon titled "Knowing and Doing," in the collection of sermons called *A Plea for the Godly*, said, "If God would only have had His laws to be *known* or *talked* of, He might have delivered them to parrots!"

Preachers must preach for conviction and change. No one ought ever to leave a sermon without having a very real sense that there is something in his life he needs to do something about. He might say, "I'm not going to do that!" But he should not be able to say, "I don't know what I'm supposed to do with that information." Shame on ministers if this happens!

The Puritan Thomas Taylor challenged ministers to preach with authority:

The word of God must be delivered in such a manner that the majesty and authority of it shall be preserved. The ambassadors of Christ must speak His message even as He himself would utter it. A flattering ministry is an enemy to this authority; for when a minister must sing placebos and sweet songs, it is impossible for him not to betray the truth.

Likewise, Taylor called upon those who sit under authoritative preaching to receive it with submission:

To withstand this authority, or to weaken it, is a fearful sin, whether in high or low men. . . . Hearers must . . . not refuse to yield subjection to this authority, nor be angry when it bears down upon some practice which they are loath to part with.

Preach the Word! Don't preach the latest fad in pop psychology. Don't preach the latest theological quirk. Don't be guilty of stealing other men's sermons. You can preach with authority only when you are confident of the material, and if your confidence is in another man so much that you constantly borrow his material, your confidence won't be in the Word.

Show your confidence in God's Word by preaching the Word. How are the people ever going to have confidence in God's Word if their minister doesn't have it? Why should they turn to it for answers when their leader doesn't? They will develop greater confidence in the Word when it is preached with conviction and authority. May God once again raise up a generation of godly preachers who will declare His Word with all its inherent authority as the very words of God Himself.

Endnotes

---

[1] Unless otherwise indicated, Scripture quotations in this chapter are from the New American Standard Version.

[2] Richard Baxter, *The Reformed Pastor*, abridged edition (1829; repr. Edinburgh, Banner of Truth Trust, 1974), 70.

Chapter 9

* * *

EVANGELISTIC PREACHING

Eric J. Alexander

$\mathscr{A}$s we approach the subject of evangelistic preaching, I think it is important to clarify two related issues.

The first is closely tied to our basic belief in the authority and sufficiency of the
whole Word of God; namely, that *the whole Bible has saving and sanctifying power.*
Consequently, we should not be surprised when people are truly converted when
we preach a part of the Bible that we would not readily classify as "evangelistic." We
regularly need to relearn Paul's great statement in 2 Timothy 3:16: "All Scripture is
God-breathed and profitable. . . ."[1]

My friend and mentor, the Rev. William Still of Aberdeen, used to tell the story
of a lady who came to his vestry before the evening service one Sunday to tell him
that her niece was with her, and she wanted her to be converted. "That means you
will have to preach the gospel tonight!" she added, and flounced out of the room.
Rev. Still happened to be preaching through Romans 9–11 at the time, and was not
inclined to be diverted. As the aunt seethed with anger in her pew at this "lecture on
the Jews," as she described it, her niece was being converted beside her.

The lesson is not that the next time you are called upon to preach on an
"evangelistic occasion" you should necessarily turn to Romans 9–11. The lesson is
rather that you need to remind yourself that God is pleased to use His *whole Word*
to accomplish the salvation of sinners.

The second issue that we must keep before us constantly in evangelistic
preaching is closely related to the first. It is that *salvation is the work of God the
Holy Spirit.* It is so easy for us to slip into a line of thinking that says, "If I just

123

arrange an evangelistic service and emphasize certain basic truths from the Bible in my preaching, people will come to faith in Christ." It is of paramount importance here, and in every other sphere of our ministry, to recognize that salvation is the sovereign work of God.

Left to ourselves, there are many things of which we are capable: we can persuade people intellectually; we can arouse and inspire them emotionally; and we can win them to ourselves psychologically. But the one thing we cannot do is to regenerate them spiritually. That task is exclusively God's.

When one of my friends, who had been in the pastorate for many fruitful years, was asked by some seminary students, "What, in your experience, is the best and most effective evangelistic method?" he replied, after some thought, "Prayer— persistent, believing prayer."

Now, if you think about it, that reply does not come from some profound theological insight. Rather, it comes from a foundational truth. If only God can save, then to whom do we turn to see our friends brought to salvation? The logical answer is, "To God!" The awkward question that sometimes follows is: "Then why is it that in most ministries and churches, prayer is supplemental rather than fundamental?" This is the background against which we need to think about evangelistic preaching.

Motivations for Evangelistic Preaching

At this point, I want to turn to the apostle Paul's second epistle to the Corinthians, where we read:

> Since, then, we know what it is to fear the Lord, we try to persuade men. What we are is plain to God, and I hope it is also plain to your conscience. We are not trying to commend ourselves to you again, but are giving you an opportunity to take pride in us, so that you can answer those who take pride in what is seen rather than in what is in the heart. If we are out of our mind, it is for the sake of God; if we are in our right mind, it is for you. For Christ's love compels us, because we are convinced that one died for all, and therefore all died. And he died for all, that those who live should no longer live for themselves but for him who died for them and was raised again.

So from now on we regard no one from a worldly point of view. Though we once regarded Christ in this way, we do so no longer. Therefore, if anyone is in Christ, he is a new creation; the old has gone, the new has come! All this is from God, who reconciled us to himself through Christ and gave us the ministry of reconciliation: that God was reconciling the world to himself in Christ, not counting men's sins against them. And he has committed to us the message of reconciliation. We are therefore Christ's ambassadors, as though God were making his appeal through us. We implore you on Christ's behalf: Be reconciled to God. God made him who had no sin to be sin for us, so that in him we might become the righteousness of God. (5:11–21)

Second Corinthians is often thought to be one of Paul's most personal letters. It reveals that he had been under great pastoral and personal stress. He had been the object of serious criticism regarding his integrity, his true motivation in preaching the gospel, and even the soundness of his mind. It should not surprise us, therefore, that in the first few verses of this passage, Paul defends his integrity and clarifies his motives as a preacher of the gospel.

In verse 9, Paul sets down the ultimate goal that directs both his life and his work: "We make it our goal to please him." Then, in verses 11 and 14, he explains the motivations of his preaching: in verse 11, it is the fear of God, and in verse 14, it is the love of Christ. Let's look at them in order:

• *The Fear of God.* The fear of the Lord is the proper reaction of creatures to God's infinite majesty and of sinners to God's infinite holiness. As we grow in the knowledge of God, we learn to tremble before His great glory and burning purity; this fear is the beginning of wisdom.

This fear has to do with an awareness of inevitable judgment. In 2 Corinthians 5:10, Paul refers to his own appearance before the judgment seat of Christ, as well as to the eventual appearance of the Corinthians at that same judgment seat. His great burden for unbelievers is that they might not come to this great and awesome day and find themselves unprepared and in utter confusion.

Now, notice what the fear of the Lord and impending judgment do for Paul's evangelism. He does not say, "Since we know what it is to fear the Lord, we frighten men." Rather he says, "Since . . . we know what it is to fear the Lord, we try to persuade men." Luke uses the same language when he describes Paul's visit to Corinth: "Every Sabbath he reasoned in the synagogue, trying to persuade Jews and Greeks" (Acts 18:4).

There is a very important principle for gospel preaching in Paul's and Luke's vocabulary. The old order of sin makes its approach and appeal through the appetite (think of the fruit of the tree in the garden, which appealed to the eyes and the appetite), whereas the new order of grace makes its appeal through the mind (think of God appealing to the people in Isaiah 1:18: "'Come, now, let us reason together,' says the LORD"). Confirmation of this principle comes in the language Luke uses to describe the apostolic preaching in Acts. He employs terms such as *didaschein* ("teach"), *dialegesthai* ("argue"), *paratithemi* ("prove"), and *syzetein* ("dispute"). Correspondingly, when people are converted, they are often said to have been "persuaded."

This does not mean that apostolic evangelism sought a mere intellectual conquest. The ultimate aim was that men and women might repent, believe, and surrender to the lordship of Jesus Christ over the whole of life. But the *approach* was through the mind. As John R. W. Stott puts it tersely, "There is no doubt that the early apostolic *kerygma* was full of solid *didache*."[2]

• *The Love of Christ.* In 2 Corinthians 5:14, Paul comes to the second main motive of his evangelistic preaching: "Christ's love compels us." It is, I think, beyond dispute that Paul is referring not to the apostles' love for Christ, but to Christ's love for them. That love had brought them under "a compulsion" or "a constraint," which (according to one translation) "leaves us no option." The word does not so much have the idea of "driving out" as "hedging around" or "holding in."

The best illustration for this that I have ever heard came from the Rev. Alan Stibbs, a one-time lecturer in New Testament at Oakhill College. He had been a missionary with the China Inland Mission and described to us the course of the Yangtze River at one point in its eastward trek. On either bank there were high, solid rocks that "constrained" the river in three ways. First, these rocks gave the river unusual depth, since the flow of the water was held in and dug deeply into the riverbed. Second, because the river was constrained by the rocks and was so deep, it had significant drive. Today, this drive is harnessed for the production of hydro-electric power. Third, the embankment created by the rocks guided the river, giving it direction. As Stibbs pointed out to us, few eras in the church's life have so badly needed depth, drive, and direction as our own. The love of Christ should motivate us in these ways as it did the apostle Paul.

It is important to notice, however, that there is nothing vague or general in Paul's reference to the love of Christ. Verse 14 makes it clear that Paul is talking about His love as uniquely manifested in His death, and indeed in a particular understanding of that death: "Christ's love compels us, because we are convinced that one died for all." The apostolic understanding of the death of Christ includes at least four elements. First, it is substitutionary in its nature (one died for all, that is, in the place of all). Second, it is penal in its character (see v. 21, which is a reference to the punishment of the sin of one being transferred to another in the world of Old Testament sacrifices). Third, it is effectual in its achievement (read verse 14: "For Christ's love compels us, because we are convinced that one died for all, and therefore all died." That is, all those for whom He died, died in Him). In short, Jesus was an effective substitute; His death in our place actually achieved our salvation. Fourth, Christ's death is revolutionary in its outcome (read v. 15). By our union with Jesus Christ, we die in His death to all that belongs to our past life, and we are raised with Him into a new life. So we cease living for ourselves and start living instead for Him who died for us and was raised again. That is why Paul is able to say in verse 17 that "if anyone is in Christ, he is a new creation."

The Ministry of Reconciliation

Paul's evangelistic preaching illustrates the use of a number of metaphors that are familiar to readers of the Epistles. They are all "picture words" drawn from various spheres of life, and they help us to understand the meaning of Christ's death.

Sometimes he uses language drawn from the law court, such as the word *justification*. There the problem is the guilt and condemnation man discovers when He is brought before God as his Judge. What Christ achieves for him by His death is a reversal of the verdict of "guilty," and the assurance that "there is now no condemnation to those who are in Christ Jesus" (Rom. 8:1).

Sometimes Paul borrows from the commercial world, using terms such as *redemption*, which carries the idea of a slave in the slave market, bound in chains and waiting for someone to pay the price of liberation. Christ is then the One who pays our ransom price and redeems us by His blood, that is, by His death.

Here in 2 Corinthians 5, Paul uses a much more familiar metaphor. It is the metaphor of reconciliation, behind which there lies the idea of man being separated and alienated from God. We use this word widely today in reference to alienation in the domestic and personal world, the national and international world, and the world of racial relations. In all these spheres, we recognize the great need for reconciliation. But Paul is persuading us that the ultimate alienation is not between man and woman, between one societal group and another, or between one race and another, but between man and God. This is the ultimate human tragedy: we are, by our sinful nature, alienated from God.

The miracle of the gospel is that God reconciles us to Himself through Jesus Christ by making our sin Christ's and by making His righteousness ours. That is what Paul is referring to in verse 21: "God made him who had no sin to be sin for us, so that in him we might become the righteousness of God." This is the glorious work of reconciliation that God has achieved through Christ. It is His work and His alone (v. 18). Archbishop Temple once said that the only thing we contribute to our salvation is the sin that makes it necessary.

But in verse 18, Paul speaks not only of the gift of salvation that God gives us in Christ, but of the gift of the *ministry of reconciliation*, which involves us carrying the message of reconciliation to the world (v. 19). It is on account of this task that Paul gives us the lofty title of "Christ's ambassadors." The privilege of this ministry is multiplied when we realize that whereas God achieved the reconciliation through Christ (v. 18), He appeals to men and women through us (v. 20). Just as Christ is the Agent for procuring the reconciliation, we are the agents for proclaiming it: "We are therefore Christ's ambassadors, as though God were making his appeal through us. We implore you on Christ's behalf: Be reconciled to God." God's entrusting of this role to human beings is one of the great mysteries of the universe. What an amazing calling! What an incredible privilege!

Principles for Evangelistic Preaching

Finally, let me set out five timeless principles that should guide our evangelistic preaching:

1. The Word of God, Holy Scripture, is our only infallible authority for the substance of the gospel message.

2. The gospel's theme is Jesus Christ as the only Savior of sinners (cf. Peter's preaching in Acts 2).

3. The Christ who saves is the Christ who is revealed to us in the whole of Scripture. Therefore, we should find the Holy Spirit convicting and saving sinners through the message of the whole Bible. This is precisely the example Jesus Himself gives us in Luke 24:27, on the road to Emmaus: "Beginning with Moses and all the Prophets, he explained to them what was said in all the Scriptures concerning himself."

4. The Bible does not save us. Christ saves us. But the only Christ who saves is the Christ who is revealed in the Bible.

5. The preaching of the gospel has two elements in it, as is apparent from the passage we have been studying. One is proclamation ("God was reconciling the world to himself in Christ"). The other is appeal ("as though God were making his appeal through us"). As Stott points out, there must be no proclamation without appeal and no appeal without proclamation.[3]

My suspicion is that while most of us would be confident that we know what the proclamation involves, we may be less clear about the nature of the appeal. This is partly because the word *appeal* has become associated with a procedure seen in crusades and missions in many parts of the world. Whatever we may think of that kind of public "going forward," it is certainly not what Paul is referring to. What he is speaking about is an appeal to the heart and conscience of his hearers to receive by repentance and faith the riches of God's saving grace in Jesus Christ. We need to press upon our hearers the necessity of heeding that appeal.

The Scriptures affirm that both repentance and faith are gifts of God. But we should be quick to add that God does not repent or believe *for* us. He implores us and earnestly appeals to us to believe on the Lord Jesus Christ. But it is we sinners who exercise saving faith, having been enabled to believe by God.

Unless I am mistaken, it is this pleading and imploring that are sometimes lacking among those of us who are called to be preachers of the gospel in the twenty-first century. May God raise up in our generation a great company of men who are constrained by the love of Christ, men who will be biblical, Christ-centered, Spirit-anointed ambassadors for Christ, combining a single-minded zeal for the glory of God with an earnest longing for the salvation of the lost.

1   All Scripture quotations in this chapter are from the New International Version.

2   John R. W. Stott. *The Preacher's Portrait* (London: Tyndale Press, 1961), 49.

3   Ibid., 48–50.

■ ■ ■

Chapter 10

PREACHING TO SUFFERING PEOPLE

John Piper

I begin with five assumptions. Without them, what I have to say about preaching and suffering will not stand.

1. Preaching is expository exultation.

2. Preaching is a normative event in the gathered church.

3. The aim of preaching is the glory of God through Jesus Christ.

4. God is most glorified in our people when our people are most satisfied in Him.

5. Suffering is a universal human experience, designed by God for His glory, but endangering every Christian's faith.

If the aim of preaching is the glory of God through Jesus Christ, and if God is most glorified in our people when they are most satisfied in Him, and if the universal human experience of suffering threatens to undermine their faith in the goodness of God, and thus their satisfaction in His glory, then our preaching must aim, week in and week out, to help our people be satisfied in God while suffering. Indeed, we must help them count suffering as part of why they should be satisfied in God. We must build into their minds and hearts a vision of God and His ways that helps them see suffering not merely as a threat to their satisfaction in God (which it is), but also as a means to their satisfaction in God (which it is). We must preach so as to make suffering seem normal and purposeful, and not surprising in this fallen age.

The forces of American culture are almost all designed to build the opposite worldview into our people's minds. Maximize comfort, ease, and security. Avoid all choices that might bring discomfort, trouble, difficulty, pain, or suffering. Add this cultural force to our natural desire for immediate gratification and fleeting pleasures, and the combined power to undermine the superior satisfaction of the soul in the glory of God through suffering is huge.

If we would see God honored in the lives of our people as the supreme value, highest treasure, and deepest satisfaction of their lives, then we must strive with all our might to show the meaning of suffering, and help them see the wisdom and power and goodness of God behind it *ordaining*; above it *governing*; beneath it *sustaining*; and before it *preparing*. This is the hardest work in the world—to change the minds and hearts of fallen human beings, and make God so precious to them that they count it all joy when trials come, and exult in their afflictions, and rejoice in the plundering of their property, and say in the end, "To die is gain."

This is why preaching is not mere communication, and why "communication theory" and getting scholarly degrees in "communication" are so far from the essence of what preaching is about. Preaching is about doing the impossible: making the rich young ruler fall out of love with his comfortable lifestyle and into love with the King of kings so that he joyfully sells all that he has to gain that treasure (Matt. 13:44). Jesus said very simply, "With men this is impossible, but with God all things are possible" (Matt. 19:26).[1] The aim of preaching is impossible; no human techniques will make it succeed. But God can work through it.

In no place does this become more clear than when preaching confronts suffering. How shall we accomplish the great end of preaching in the face of suffering?

Coming to Christ means more suffering, not less, in this world. For starters, I am persuaded that suffering is normal and not exceptional. We all will suffer; we all *must* suffer; and most American Christians are not prepared in mind or heart to believe or experience this. Therefore, the glory of God, the honor of Christ, the stability of the church, and the strength of commitment to world missions are at stake. If preaching does not help our people be satisfied in God through suffering, then God will not be glorified, Christ will not be honored, the church will be a weakling in an escapist world of ease, and the completion of the Great Commission with its demand for martyrdom will fail.

There is a certainty of suffering that will come to people if they embrace the Savior. "Teacher, I will follow You wherever You go." Really? "The foxes have holes and the birds of the air have nests, but the Son of Man has nowhere to lay His head" (Matt. 8:19–20). "Many are the afflictions of the righteous" (Ps. 34:19a); "'A slave is not greater than his master.' If they persecuted Me, they will also persecute you" (John 15:20); "If they have called the head of the house 'Beelzebul,' how much more will they malign the members of his household!" (Matt. 10:25); "Christ also suffered for you, leaving you an example for you to follow in His steps" (1 Peter 2:21); "Do not be surprised at the fiery ordeal among you, which comes upon you for your testing, as though some strange thing were happening to you" (1 Peter 4:12); "Through many tribulations we must enter the kingdom of God" (Acts 14:22); "Let no one be disturbed by these afflictions; for you yourselves know that we have been destined for this" (1 Thess. 3:3); We are "fellow heirs with Christ, if indeed we suffer with Him so that we may also be glorified with Him. For I consider that the sufferings of this present time are not worthy to be compared with the glory that is to be revealed to us" (Rom. 8:17–18); "All who desire to live godly in Christ Jesus will be persecuted" (2 Tim. 3:12); "I protest, brethren, by my pride in you which I have in Christ Jesus our Lord, I die every day!" (1 Cor. 15:31, RSV); and "If for this life only we have hoped in Christ, we are of all men most to be pitied" (1 Cor. 15:19, RSV). People are going to suffer—that is certain.

And when this life of necessary suffering is at an end, there remains the last enemy, death. "It is appointed for men to die once and after this comes judgment" (Heb. 9:27). For God's loved ones, dying will be the final suffering. For most of us it will be a terrible thing. In more than twenty-eight years in the pastorate, I have walked with many saints through the last months and days and hours of dying. And very few have been easy. Everyone I preach to is going to die if Christ delays His coming. All must suffer and all must die.

"You sweep them away as with a flood; they are like a dream, like grass. . . . In the morning it flourishes and is renewed; in the evening it fades and withers. The years of our life are seventy, or even by reason of strength eighty; yet their span is but toil and trouble; they are soon gone, and we fly away. . . . So teach us to number our days that we may get a heart of wisdom" (Ps. 90:5–12, ESV).

What does a pastoral heart of wisdom do when it discovers that death is sure, that life is short, and that suffering is inevitable and necessary? The answer is given two verses later in Psalm 90. It is a prayer: "Have pity on your servants! Satisfy us in the morning with your steadfast love, that we may rejoice and be glad all our days" (vv. 13b–14, ESV). In the face of toil, trouble, suffering, and death, the wise preacher cries out with the psalmist, "Satisfy us in the morning with Your steadfast love." He prays this both for himself and for his people: "O God, grant that we would be satisfied with Your steadfast love always, and need nothing else"—and then he preaches to that end.

Why? Because if a preacher leaves his people where they are, seeking satisfaction in family and job and leisure and toys and sex and money and food and power and esteem, when suffering and death strip it all away they will be embittered and angry and depressed. And the worth and beauty and goodness and power and wisdom of God, the glory of God, will vanish in the cloud of murmuring, complaining, and cursing.

But if the preacher has prayed well (that God would satisfy them with Himself); if the preacher has preached well (showing them that they must suffer, but that God is more to be desired than comfort and the steadfast love of the Lord is better than life (Ps. 63:3); if the preacher has lived well (rejoicing to suffer for their sakes); and if the preacher has lingered long enough in one place of ministry, then many of the people will suffer well and die well, counting it gain because they are satisfied in God alone. God will therefore be mightily glorified, and the great end of preaching will be achieved.

Preaching and the Suffering of the Preacher

If the ultimate aim of preaching is the glory of God through Jesus Christ, if God is most glorified when we are most satisfied in Him, and if suffering threatens that satisfaction in God and must come, then we should preach so as to help our people say with the psalmist, from their hearts, "The steadfast love of the Lord is better than life" (Ps. 63:3), and to say with Paul, "I count everything as loss because of the surpassing worth of knowing Christ Jesus my Lord" (Phil. 3:8, RSV). Preachers must have a passion to produce people whose satisfaction in God is so solid, so deep, and so unshakable that suffering and death—losing everything this world can give—will not make people murmur or curse God, but rest in the promise, "In His presence is fullness of joy, at His right hand are pleasures forevermore" (Ps. 16:11).

But how shall men preach like that? The answer is that the preacher must suffer and the preacher must rejoice. The preacher *himself* must be hurt in the ministry, and the preacher must be happy in God.

Follow with me the three generations of preaching from Christ through the apostle Paul to Timothy. Jesus Christ came into the world to suffer. He took on human flesh so that there would be a body to torture and kill (Heb. 2:14). Suffering was the heart of His ministry. "The Son of Man did not come to be served, but to serve, and to give His life a ransom for many" (Mark 10:45); "Though He was rich, yet for your sake He became poor so that you, through His poverty, might become rich" (2 Cor. 8:9); "Thus it is written, that the Christ should suffer and on the third day rise from the dead" (Luke 24:46, RSV); and "He began to teach them that the Son of Man must suffer many things and be rejected by the elders and the chief priests and the scribes, and be killed, and after three days rise again" (Mark 8:31). When Jesus preached, He preached as one whose suffering embodied His message. He is absolutely unique in this. His suffering was the salvation that he preached.

But even though He was unique (a preacher's suffering will never be the salvation of his people in the same way), He nevertheless calls us to join Him in this suffering. Christ then makes that suffering part of our ministry and, in great measure, the power of our message. When they wanted to follow Him, He said, "The foxes have holes, and the birds of the air have nests, but the Son of Man has nowhere to lay His head" (Matt. 8:20). In other words, "Do you really want to follow Me? Know what you were called to!" "A slave is not greater than his master. If they persecuted Me, they will also persecute you" (John 15:20); "If they have called the head of the house Beelzebul, how much more will they malign the members of his household!" (Matt. 10:25); and "As the Father has sent Me, even so I send you" (John 20:21, RSV). Or as Peter put it, "Christ also suffered for you, leaving you an example for you to follow in His steps" (1 Peter 2:21).

Specifically concerning the apostle Paul, the risen Christ said, "I will show him how much he must suffer for My name's sake" (Acts 9:16). Paul understood his own sufferings as a necessary extension of Christ's for the sake of the church. So he said to the Colossians, "I rejoice in my sufferings for your sake, and in my flesh I complete what is lacking in Christ's afflictions for the sake of His body, that is, the church" (Col. 1:24, RSV). His sufferings did not complete the atoning worth of Christ's sufferings. You can't complete perfection. They completed, rather, the extension of those sufferings in person, in a suffering representative, to those for whom Christ suffered.

Paul had to suffer in the ministry of the gospel. It was an essential extension of the sufferings of Christ. Why? Besides extending the sufferings of Christ in Paul's own suffering to others, there are other reasons. One of his testimonies gives another answer: "For we do not want you to be unaware, brethren, of our affliction which came to us in Asia, that we were burdened excessively, beyond our strength, so that we despaired even of life; indeed, we had the sentence of death within ourselves so that we would not trust in ourselves, but in God who raises the dead" (2 Cor. 1:8–9). Notice the purpose of this suffering: "So that we would not trust in ourselves, but in God who raises the dead." This is not the purpose of Satan, and it is not the purpose of Paul's enemies. It is the purpose of God. God ordained the suffering of His apostle so that he would be radically and totally dependent on nothing else but God. All is about to be lost on this earth. If there is anything left to hope in, it is God alone, who raises the dead. That is all. Paul's sufferings are designed to throw him back again and again on God alone as his hope and treasure.

But that is not the end of God's purpose. Second Corinthians 1:8–9 begins with the word *for*. Paul's sufferings are meant to support what goes before, namely, the comfort of the church. Paul says this several ways. For example, verse 6: "If we are afflicted, it is for your comfort and salvation; or if we are comforted, it is for your comfort." So Paul's affliction as a minister of the Word is designed not only to throw him solely on God for his comfort, but also to bring that same comfort and salvation to the people he serves. His suffering is for their sake.

How does that work? How do Paul's sufferings help his people find their comfort and satisfaction in God alone? Paul explains it like this: "We have this treasure [the treasure of the gospel of the glory of Christ] in earthen vessels, so that the surpassing greatness of the power will be of God and not from ourselves; we are afflicted in every way, but not crushed; perplexed, but not despairing; persecuted, but not forsaken; struck down, but not destroyed" (2 Cor. 4:7–9). In other words, these terrible things happen to Paul to show that the power of his ministry is not from himself, but is God's power (v. 7). Paul's suffering is designed by God to magnify the "surpassing greatness" of God's power.

He says it again in verse 10: "Always carrying about in the body the dying of Jesus, so that the life of Jesus also may be manifested in our body." In other words, Paul shares in the sufferings of Christ in order to display the life of Jesus more clearly. The aim of the ministry of the preacher is to display Christ, to show that

He is more to be desired than all earthly comforts and pleasures. And the suffering of the preacher is designed to make clear that Christ is in fact that valuable, that precious. "I die daily," he says, "so that the surpassing value of Christ will be seen in my suffering body." This is how it works. This is how Paul's sufferings help his people find their comfort and satisfaction in God alone.

Paul says it again in 2 Corinthians 12:9. When he implores the Lord to take away the painful thorn in the flesh, Christ answers, "My grace is sufficient for you, for power is perfected in weakness." And Paul responds, "Most gladly, therefore, I will rather boast about my weaknesses, so that the power of Christ may dwell in me. Therefore I am well content with weaknesses, with insults, with distresses, with persecutions, with difficulties, for Christ's sake; for when I am weak, then I am strong." Paul's thorn in the flesh was to humble Paul and magnify the all-sufficiency of the grace of Christ.

So the suffering of the apostle displayed the "surpassing greatness" of the power of God (2 Cor. 4:7), the triumph of the "life of Jesus" (2 Cor. 4:10), and the perfection of "the grace of Christ" (2 Cor. 12:9). When the people saw this in the suffering of the apostle Paul, it causes them to treasure Christ as more precious than life, which produces a radically transformed life to the glory of God.

Paul explains this dynamic in 2 Corinthians 3:18: "And we all, with unveiled face, beholding the glory of the Lord, are being changed into His likeness from one degree of glory to another" (RSV). Beholding is becoming. When we see Him for who He really is in His glory, our hearts cherish Him, and thus magnify Him, and we are changed. Everything changes. That is the goal of preaching. And that is the goal of the suffering of the preacher.

Paul puts it in one cryptic sentence in 2 Corinthians 4:12: "Death works in us, but life in you." Suffering, weakness, calamity, and hardship work death in Paul, and in so doing show that the surpassing greatness of his ministry belongs to Christ, not to him. And that manifestation of the surpassing worth of Christ works life in those who see, because life comes from seeing and savoring Christ as our highest treasure.

So Christ comes to preach and to suffer. His suffering and death are the heart of His message. Then He appears to Paul and tells him how much he must suffer in the ministry of the gospel—not because Paul's suffering and death is the content of his message, Christ's is. But because, in his suffering, Christ's suffering is seen and presented to those for whom He suffered, and His glory shines with surpassing value as the greatest treasure of the universe.

Then, when Paul undertakes to help Timothy (and us), what does he say? He says, by way of example, in 2 Timothy 2:10, "I endure everything for the sake of the elect, that they also may obtain salvation in Christ Jesus with its eternal glory" (RSV). God's assignment for him as a minister of the Word is to suffer for the elect.

Then he turns to Timothy and gives him the same calling, which is why I believe it applies to us. "Timothy, making disciples will cost you dearly." Second Timothy 2:2–3: "The things which you have heard from me in the presence of many witnesses, entrust these to faithful men who will be able to teach others also. Suffer hardship with me, as a good soldier of Christ Jesus." Entrust the word to others, Timothy. The price: "Suffer hardship with me."

But what about preaching in particular? Paul addresses the issue directly in 2 Timothy 4:2–5: "Preach the Word; be ready in season and out of season; reprove, rebuke, exhort, with great patience and instruction. For the time will come when they will not endure sound doctrine; but wanting to have their ears tickled, they will accumulate for themselves teachers in accordance to their own desires, and will turn away their ears from the truth and will turn aside to myths. But you, be sober in all things, endure hardship." Preach the word, endure hardship! Preach the Word, Timothy. The price? Endure hardship.

We must preach with a passion to produce people whose satisfaction in God is so solid, so deep, and so unshakable that suffering and death will not make our people murmur or curse God, but will help them count it all joy (James 1:2) and say with Paul, "To live is Christ and to die is gain" (Phil. 1:21). How will that happen? I said that the preacher must suffer. That is what I have tried to show thus far. And then the preacher must rejoice. He must be hurt in the ministry, *and* he must be happy in God.

Of course, Paul commands this of all of us. "Rejoice in the Lord always; again I say, rejoice" (Phil. 4:4). "We exult in hope of the glory of God. And not only this, but we also exult in our tribulations" (Rom. 5:2–3). It is crucial to see how Paul speaks of his own experience in suffering in the ministry of the Word. He does not just say to the Colossians, "I suffer for your sake." He says, "I rejoice in my sufferings for your sake" (Col. 1:24). He doesn't just say to the

Corinthians, "I boast about my weaknesses." He says, "Most gladly, therefore, will I boast about my weaknesses" (2 Cor. 12:9). Yes, there is sorrow, sometimes almost unbearable sorrow. But even here he says, "as sorrowful, yet always rejoicing" (2 Cor. 6:10). And when he writes to the Thessalonians to commend them for their faith, he says, "You also became imitators of us and of the Lord, having received the Word in much tribulation with the joy of the Holy Spirit" (1 Thess. 1:6).

Why this stress on joy in the Lord, joy in the hope of the glory of God, joy from the Holy Spirit, and all in the midst of suffering? The reason is this: The aim of preaching is the glory of God through Jesus Christ. God is most glorified in us when we are most satisfied in Him. But suffering is a great threat to our satisfaction in God. We are tempted to murmur, complain, blame, and even to curse and quit the ministry. Therefore, joy in God in the midst of suffering makes the worth of God—the all-satisfying glory of God—shine more brightly than it would through our joy at any other time. Sunshine happiness signals the value of sunshine. But happiness in suffering signals the value of God. Suffering and hardship joyfully accepted in the path of obedience to Christ show the supremacy of Christ more than all our faithfulness in fair days.

When a preacher preaches with this joy and this suffering, the people will see Christ for the infinite treasure that He is, and, as a result of this seeing, will cherish Him above all things and thus be changed from one degree of glory to the next. The glory of God will be magnified in the church and in the world, and the great aim of preaching will be achieved.

Preaching and the Suffering of the People

Suffering will come to believers. It must come. It is part of their calling. In Philippians 1:29, Paul tells the entire church in Philippi, "To you it has been granted for Christ's sake not only to believe in Him, but also to suffer for His sake." This is a gift from God to all believers. We are appointed to suffer. "You yourselves know that we have been destined for this" (1 Thess. 3:3). We are preaching to disciples of Jesus, not disciples of Hugh Hefner. "Can we wish, if it were possible, to walk in a path strewed with flowers when His was strewed with thorns?"[2]

For the glory of God to be manifest in our people's lives, they must rejoice in suffering rather than murmur and complain. This is why the Bible tells them again and again, "Blessed are you when men revile you . . . rejoice and be glad" (Matt. 5:11–12, RSV); "We rejoice in our sufferings, knowing that suffering produces endurance" (Rom. 5:3, RSV); "Count it all joy . . . when you meet various trials" (James 1:2); "Rejoice in so far as you share Christ's sufferings" (1 Peter 4:13, RSV); "You joyfully accepted the plundering of your property" (Heb. 10:34, RSV); and "They left the presence of the council, rejoicing that they were counted worthy to suffer dishonor for the name" (Acts 5:41, RSV).

People are not prepared or able to rejoice in suffering unless they experience a massive biblical revolution of how they think and feel about the meaning of life. Human nature and American culture make it impossible to rejoice in suffering. This is a miracle in the human soul wrought by God through His Word. It is the aim of preaching to be the agent of God in bringing about that miracle through the Word.

Jesus said to Peter at the end of John's Gospel, "'When you grow old, you will stretch out your hands and someone else will gird you, and bring you where you do not wish to go.' Now this He said, signifying by what kind of death he would glorify God" (John 21:18–19). In other words, God appoints a kind of suffering and death by which each of us is called to glorify God. And since the great aim of preaching is the glory of God, we must preach to prepare people to suffer and die like that.

It is important, then, for preachers to understand how their own suffering affects their preaching for the sake of their suffering people.

First, God has ordained that our preaching becomes deeper and more winsome as we are broken, humbled, and made low and desperately dependent on grace by the trials of our lives. Jesus said it about His own ministry like this: "Come to Me, all who labor and are heavy laden, and I will give you rest. Take My yoke upon you, and learn from Me; for I am gentle and lowly in heart, and you will find rest for your souls" (Matt. 11:28–29, RSV). People will come and learn from us how to suffer if we are "gentle and lowly in heart." And that is what our sufferings are designed to make us. Paul writes, "We were so utterly, unbearably crushed that we despaired of life itself . . . [so that we would] rely not on ourselves but on God who raises the dead" (2 Cor. 1:8–9, RSV). God aims to break us of all pretenses to self-sufficiency, and make us lowly and childlike in our dependence on Him. This is the kind of preacher to whom the suffering comes.

John Newton wrote to a fellow pastor and said,

> It belongs to your calling of God as a minister, that you should have a taste of the various spiritual trials which are incident to the Lord's people, that thereby you may . . . know how to speak a word in season to them that are weary; and it is likewise needful to keep you perpetually attentive to that important admonition, "Without Me ye can do nothing."[3]

It is true that we must be bold in the pulpit and afraid of no man but courageous as we contend for the truth. But it is just as true that our boldness must be brokenhearted boldness, that our courage must be a contrite and lowly courage, and that we must be tender contenders for the truth. If we are brash and harsh and cocky and clever, we may win a hearing with angry and pugnacious people, but we will drive away those who suffer. Paul makes it so clear that we are laid low and given comfort "so that we will be able to comfort those who are in any affliction with the comfort with which we ourselves are comforted by God" (2 Cor. 1:4). It must feel to our people that we are utterly dependent in our lives on the merciful comfort of God to make it through our days.

Second, God has ordained that when we preach from weakness and suffering sustained by joy in Christ, the people see that Christ is treasured and they are loved. Here we are up against a huge obstacle in American culture. The twentieth century was the century of the self. Almost all virtues, especially love, were reinterpreted to put the self at the center. This means that almost all our people are saturated and shaped with the conviction that the essence of being loved as a human is being treasured or esteemed. That is, you love me to the degree that your act of treasuring terminates on me.

But God ordains the suffering of preachers to show the all-surpassing worth of Jesus because we treasure Christ as we preach to our people. And if they ask, "Do you treasure me or do you treasure Christ?" I answer, "I treasure Christ, and, desiring to treasure Him more, I treasure your treasuring Christ." Without the miraculous work of the Holy Spirit removing human self from the center, this will not satisfy American people. They are so saturated with self-oriented love that they can scarcely conceive what true Christian love is. True Christian love is not my making much of them, but my helping them to enjoy making much of God. This is love. If my treasuring terminates on them, I play right into the hands of the Devil and their own self-centered destruction. But if my treasuring terminates on God and their treasuring God, then I direct them to the one source of all joy. And that act of directing them to God, their hope and life and joy, is what love is.

Our aim in preaching is not to help our people feel treasured, but to help them treasure God. We must aim to preach in such a way that we breed a kind of people who feel loved not when they are made much of, but when they are patiently helped to enjoy making much of God, even when they themselves are slandered, ridiculed, persecuted, and killed. This is impossible with man, but with God all things are possible. When the Holy Spirit comes in power on our preaching, people see that Christ is treasured and they are loved, and that those two things are one. God has ordained that one way they see Christ treasured in us is how we are sustained by Him in suffering.

Third, the suffering of the preacher helps him see from Scripture what he must say to his suffering people. Martin Luther made the point powerfully and straight out of the Bible, not just from experience. He cites Psalm 119:67 and 71: "Before I was afflicted I went astray, but now I keep Thy word. . . . It is good for me that I was afflicted, that I may learn Thy statutes." Here Luther found an indispensable key for the preacher in unlocking texts. "It was good for me that I was afflicted, that I may learn Your statutes." There are things to see in the Word of God that our eyes can only see through the lens of tears.

Luther said it this way: "I want you to know how to study theology in the right way. I have practiced this method myself. . . . Here you will find three rules. They are frequently proposed throughout Psalm [119] and run thus: *Oratio, meditatio, tentatio* (prayer, meditation, tribulation)."[4] And tribulations he called the "touchstone." They "teach you not only to know and understand, but also to experience how right, how true, how sweet, how lovely, how mighty, how comforting God's Word is; it is wisdom supreme."[5]

He proved the value of suffering over and over again in his own experience. "For as soon as God's Word becomes known through you, the devil will afflict you, will make a real doctor of you, and will teach you by his temptations to seek and to love God's Word. For I myself . . . owe my papists many thanks for so beating, pressing, and frightening me through the devil's raging that they have turned me into a fairly good theologian, driving me to a goal I should never have reached."[6]

Luther calls it theology. I call it preaching. In other words, Psalm 119:71 teaches us that the suffering of the preacher opens to him the Scriptures in a way he would not otherwise know them, and so shows him in the Scriptures what to say to his people, mingled with how to say it.

The first thing you will learn to say to your people is that they must suffer. You will make it a theme running through all your messages: They will get sick; they will be persecuted; and they will die. They must be reminded of these things again and again, because almost all forces in the culture are pushing them away from these realities and trying to get them not to think about it and therefore not to be ready for it, and certainly not value it when it comes. However, when suffering teaches you the meaning of Scripture, you will learn and preach that all suffering is of one piece, and that saints will taste all of it—sickness, persecution, and death.

You will show them from Romans 8:23 that they will get sick. "We ourselves, having the firstfruits of the Spirit, even we ourselves groan within ourselves, waiting eagerly for our adoption as sons, the redemption of our body." Yes, you will teach them to pray for their healing, but you also will teach them that the full and final blood-bought healing of Christ is for the age to come when all crying and pain and tears will be no more (Rev. 21:4). In this age we groan, waiting for the redemption of our bodies. Here the outer nature is wasting away while our inner nature is being renewed day by day (2 Cor. 4:16). We will preach this and give our people a theology of sickness.

And we will preach that persecution, whether small or large, must come. "Indeed, all who desire to live godly in Christ Jesus will be persecuted" (2 Tim. 3:12). You will balance with warning the caution that they not seek to provoke offense. The gospel and the path of sacrifice and the cause of truth are the offense, not the cranky personalities of the saints. The aim is to treasure Christ above all things, and to love people with the truth no matter the cost. That will bring the trouble. We must preach to motivate our people and prepare them.

We will preach that they all must die, and we will bend every effort to help them say, when the time comes, "To die is gain." If we can help them value Christ above all that death will take away, they will be the freest and most radical, sacrificial people in the world.

Not only must we preach that all people will get sick, be persecuted, and die, but also that God is sovereign and designs all their suffering for their everlasting good. Newton is right again when he says that one of Satan's main devices against God's people is to hide from them the Lord's designs in permitting him thus to rage.[7] Preaching should not hide these designs, but reveal them. That is how we will establish our people and give them hope and joy in suffering. They must know and cherish the truth that their adversaries (natural and supernatural) mean it for evil, but God means it for good (Gen. 50:20).

Some people will stumble over the word *"designs,"* that God actually *plans* the suffering of His people and therefore has good designs in it. William Barclay (an old-line liberal from a generation ago) represents many when he says, "I believe that pain and suffering are never the will of God for His children."[8] There are open theists today who teach, "God does not have a specific divine purpose for each and every occurrence of evil."[9] Or, as one says: "When an individual inflicts pain on another individual, I do not think we can go looking for 'the purpose of God' in the event. . . . I know Christians frequently speak about 'the purpose of God' in the midst of a tragedy caused by someone else. . . . But this I regard to simply be a piously confused way of thinking."[10]

Do not preach that to your people and undermine their biblical hope. Their hope is this—and you will see it most clearly and say it most sweetly when you have experienced it most deeply—that all their suffering is the discipline of their Father for their good (Heb. 12:11); it is the refining fire of faith (1 Peter 1:7); it is the crucible of perseverance and character and hope (Rom. 5:3–4); it is the preparation of an eternal weight of glory beyond all comparison (2 Cor. 4:17). And if they will believe and rejoice, it is the display of the supreme value of Christ when your people say, "The steadfast love of the LORD is better than life" (Ps. 63:3). It is not by accident, but by design, that all wise people confess with Malcolm Muggeridge, who, at the end of his life, said: "Looking over my 90 years, I realize I have never made any progress in good times. I only progressed in the hard times."[11] When we experience this, we are more alert to it in Scripture, and when we see it, we preach it for our suffering people.

There is one last connection between the preacher's suffering and the suffering of his people, namely, that his suffering will show him that the timing of teaching and touching is crucial. "There is a time for everything . . . a time to weep, and a time to laugh; a time to mourn, and a time to dance; . . . a time to embrace, and a time to refrain from embracing; . . . a time to keep silence, and a time to speak" (Eccl. 3:1, 4–7, RSV). Preaching involves timing. Preach the whole truth about suffering and the sovereign goodness of God while it is day, and when the night comes and you stand beside the suicide victim's pool of blood or the ice-cold, ivory body of a one-year-old boy, you won't have to say anything. This will be a time for embracing. At this point the suffering saints will be glad that your suffering has taught you to preach the hard things and then, at the right time, to be silent.

When you walk through your own valley of darkness, you learn these things. This is your lifelong seminary. If you are called to preach, I entreat you, do not begrudge the seminary of suffering.

Endnotes

1   Unless otherwise indicated, all Scripture quotations in this chapter are from the New American Standard Version.

2   John Newton, *The Works of John Newton* (Edinburgh: Banner of Truth Trust, 1985), 1:230.

3   Ibid., 1:255.

4   Ewald M. Plass, *What Luther Says* (St. Louis: Concordia, 1959), 3:1359.

5   Ibid., 1360.

6   Ibid.

7   Newton, *The Works of John Newton*, 1:233.

8   William Barclay, *A Spiritual Autobiography* (Grand Rapids: Eerdmans, 1975), 44.

9   John Sanders, *The God Who Risks: A Theology of Providence* (Downers Grove, Ill.: InterVarsity, 1998), 262.

10 Greg Boyd, *Letters from a Skeptic: A Son Wrestles with His Father's Questions about Christianity* (Colorado Springs, Colo.: Chariot Victor, 1994), 46–47.

11 Quoted in Fred Smith, "Mentored by the Prince of Preachers," *Leadership* (Summer 1992), 54.

Chapter 11

■ ■ ■

A REMINDER TO SHEPHERDS

John MacArthur

*Y*ears ago, a magazine called *New West* premiered here in California. The first issue featured an article about Christians on television. The journalist wrote a line at the end of his article that I'll never forget: "Personally, I assume Jesus has more class than most of His agents."

He was right. Jesus definitely has more class than *all* of His agents. It is an old adage that you can't tell the value of something by the package it comes in. That is certainly true of preachers and of the rest of us who are witnesses to the gospel of Jesus Christ. Like the pearl without price hidden in the ugly oyster shell, the container doesn't always reflect the value of its contents.[1]

The apostle Paul makes that very point in 2 Corinthians 4. Often I am asked to sign a Bible or one of my books, and when I do so I write "2 Corinthians 4:5–7" under my name, because this is a passage in which I find my life and ministry defined. The passage says: "For we do not preach ourselves but Christ Jesus as Lord, and ourselves as your bond-servants for Jesus' sake. For God, who said, 'Light shall shine out of darkness,' is the One who has shone in our hearts to give the light of the knowledge of the glory of God in the face of Christ. But we have this treasure in earthen vessels, that the surpassing greatness of the power may be of God and not from ourselves."[2] Here we see the amazing contrast between the shining glory of God in the face of Jesus Christ and the feeble, imperfect, fragile, ugly containers by which this glorious gospel is carried and delivered to people.

Let me give some background. When Paul founded the Corinthian church, I don't think he had any idea how much these people would break his heart. First of all, they broke his heart by dragging into their lives as Christians all the sins for which they had been forgiven in their justification. So he wrote his first letter to them, pointing out numerous iniquities that were characteristics of their pre-Christian life and urging them to shed those things. It wasn't long after he had unburdened his grieving heart over their sin that false teachers came into the church and brought doctrines of demons. Paul called these heretical teachers hypocritical liars. The first thing on their agenda when they arrived in Corinth was the elevation of their own status—and they sought ascendency for themselves at Paul's expense. They needed recognition (and believability) as teachers. In order to gain that, they had to destroy the people's confidence in their spiritual father, Paul. So they assaulted Paul relentlessly, mercilessly, and consistently. For months and months they attacked him in ways calculated to undermine his credibility, integrity, apostleship, and message. He was so devastated by this on one occasion that he went back to Corinth for a visit, and when he got there in an effort to straighten things out and call the Corinthians back to himself (not for his own sake, but for the sake of the truth), a man in the congregation apparently stood up and blasted Paul to his face, and when nobody defended Paul, he left with an absolutely shattered heart. He then sent Titus there with another letter (one not included in the New Testament canon) containing this message: "Don't abandon me, because if you abandon me you'll abandon the truth."

Titus returned with a good report: the people had responded positively. But Paul knew the false teachers were still there, and he feared for the future because the people were fickle, so he wrote 2 Corinthians. That epistle had to be the hardest thing for a man like Paul to write, because in it he had to defend himself as a teacher of the truth, as the apostle of Jesus Christ, and as the messenger of God—and yet he knew himself to be nothing. That is why 2 Corinthians is a masterpiece of a man walking a fine line. We get a glimpse of how Paul did that in 2 Corinthians 4:5–7.

Relentless Attacks

The false apostles were ruthless and unrelenting in their attempts to discredit Paul. They attacked him with every accusation they could dream up. Therefore, he begins his defense by saying, "Since we have this ministry, as we received mercy, we do not lose heart" (v. 1). This was an echo of a famous statement in his first epistle to that church: "I am what I am by the grace of God" (1 Cor. 15:10). Paul was reminding himself that both his ministry and his salvation were mercies he didn't deserve anyway. That self-reminder became the encouragement he clung to in the face of such a vicious attack.

Paul goes on to say that he and his companions have renounced the things hidden because of shame (v. 2). The false teachers apparently were saying that if the Corinthians really knew Paul, they would know he was a hypocrite and a deceiver. *On the surface,* they said, *he seems religious, holy, sanctified, and pious; but the fact of the matter is that he has a secret life of shame.* These were vicious and utterly unwarranted accusations, but persistent talk like that threatened to destroy his reputation—and that in turn was undermining the Corinthians' confidence in what they had learned from Paul.

So he assured them he was not "walking in craftiness" (v. 2). This was a simple, direct answer to the main insinuation of all their complaints against him: *He is a manipulator, a con man.* The word translated in 2:17 as "peddling" had deliberate connotations of hucksterism. Paul responds, "I am no charlatan!" They also claimed Paul had adulterated the Word, and he categorically denies that charge as well, stating that he and his team declared the truth in such a way as to commend themselves to everyone's consciences. If Paul sounds self-protective, remember that he was directly countering allegations these false teachers had spread around against him. But he was doing this not for his own sake—rather, it was for the defense of the gospel, which would lose its foothold in Corinth if these heretics had their way.

As if attacking his character and theology were not enough, the false teachers even attacked Paul personally. They liberally employed *ad hominem* arguments, trying to destroy the man himself. They said his personal presence was unimpressive and his speech was downright contemptible (10:10). In other words, he was ugly and couldn't communicate. That is really bad! If you're handsome, even if you can't communicate, people can enjoy looking. And if you're ugly but can communicate, they can enjoy listening. But if you're ugly and can't communicate, you've got nothing! The fact that Paul even needed to reply to such attacks has led some commentators to speculate that there was something believable about them. Some go so far as to imagine Paul as a small hunchback with serious physical deformities. We *do* know he was aging and scarred. Whatever disfigurement Paul might have had, this was a terribly unkind assault on the man himself, sneering at whatever physical defects he might have had.

Paul also alluded in 1 Corinthians 1 to the fact that they said he gave a simple message about the cross over and over again, never using the wisdom of men or the great themes of philosophy. Clearly (though Paul was a true scholar) he did not show off his erudition, and he didn't try to use charm, charisma, or intellectual gimmickry to make his teaching seem more appealing. Therefore they said things like: *Paul just doesn't have what it takes. He doesn't have the persona or the philosophical relevance to step into this culture, meet it where it is, and communicate with it.*

But whatever his shortcomings were—appearance, personal charm, oratorical skills—Paul himself was fully aware of them. Notice his response: "What do you want out of a clay pot?" He turned their arguments back on them. He said: "You're right. I agree about my weaknesses. I agree about my inabilities. You can't pick a fight with me about that. I'm not here to defend myself." Like all noble ministers, he was being put in a very embarrassing position; he was being criticized by people much more sinful and weak than he was, and yet he found it very painful to defend himself because he knew he was nothing. But at the same time, he knew that the New Covenant he proclaimed was everything.

The starkness of the contrast between the glory of the message and the crudeness of the vessel used to deliver it is very apparent. Verses 5–6 blaze out at us as if we had stepped into the Holy of Holies in the tabernacle on the day the glory arrived; or as if we were standing beside Moses in Exodus when the glory of God was shown to him on Mount Sinai; or as if we were with Peter, James, and John on the Mount of Transfiguration when Jesus pulled back the veil of His flesh, and the *shekinah* blazed forth and put them into a temporary coma; or as if we were with Isaiah in the temple in Isaiah 6 when he had his vision of God that crushed him to the ground and made him confess only his sin and unworthiness; or as if we were with Ezekiel when he saw the vision of God and fainted; or as if we were with John when he saw the glorified Son in Revelation 1 and fell on his face like a dead man. Paul sees the blazing, shining reality that God in Christ, with the New Covenant, is saving sinners. He sees the blazing glory of God revealed in the face of Jesus Christ, this glorious New Covenant revelation. And then he says in verse 7, "But we have this treasure in earthen vessels." Frail, imperfect, and common that he was, he agreed with the false teachers' assessments. It never ceased to be a wonder to Paul that God would put such a priceless treasure in such a clay pot.

In 1 Timothy 1:12, Paul wrote, "I thank Christ Jesus our Lord, who strengthened me, because He considered me faithful, putting me into service." He was astounded by God's grace! He had come to the end of his life, a man in his sixties, but he remembered his life before Christ: "I was . . . a blasphemer . . . and a persecutor . . . and a violent aggressor. And yet I was shown mercy . . . and the grace of our Lord was more than abundant. . . . It is a trustworthy statement, deserving full acceptance, that Christ Jesus came into the world to save sinners, among whom I am foremost of all" (1 Tim. 1:13–15). Note that he did not say he *was* the foremost sinner, but "I am." He never got over God's grace.

God Uses Clay Pots

Preachers are men—that's all. And men are not perfect, so there is no hope of perfection in the ministry. If God could not use poor instruments and feeble voices, He couldn't make music. Abraham was guilty of duplicity, yet he became the man of faith and the friend of God. Moses was a man of stuttering speech and a quick temper, yet he was the one chosen to lead a nation, to represent them before God, and to receive His law and deliver it to them. David was guilty of adultery, conspiracy, murder, and unfaithfulness as a husband and father, but he repented and was regarded as a man after God's own heart. He was also the greatest songwriter of all history. We still sing the songs of this "sweet singer of Israel." Elijah ran from Jezebel, pleading for euthanasia, but this same Elijah defied Ahab and all the prophets of Baal, and heard the still small voice of God at Horeb. In the midst of the heavenly vision, Isaiah said, "I am a man with a dirty mouth; I live among people with dirty mouths. I'm certainly useless to you, O God." But when he had been cleansed, he said, "Here am I; send me," and God said, "Go." Peter was another clay pot, the leader and spokesman of the twelve apostles, but he denied his Lord with oaths and curses, and even had the audacity to correct the Lord. However, he was restored by the compassion of Jesus in the midst of his disobedience, and was enabled by the power of the Holy Spirit to speak with such force on the day of Pentecost as to be the agent by which God orchestrated the great introduction of the church. John the apostle expected to be praised by Jesus for refusing to allow a man not of their company to cast out demons in the name of the Lord. Likewise, he and his brother James wanted to call down fire from heaven and burn up a Samaritan village, and they sent their mother to ask that they might be given the chief places in the kingdom. Yet John became the beloved disciple, the apostle of love, the eagle who soared to great heights. He became, it seems, the apostle who pierced the deepest into the mystery of the incarnation.

Are you seeing a pattern?

So it was with Paul. He was under assault unjustly; he was falsely accused; he was battered and hammered. The attacks against him were often physical. In 2 Corinthians 11, he lists all of the physical attacks he endured: five times beaten by the Jews with thirty-nine stripes; three times beaten with rods by the Gentiles; and once stoned. Then there were the criticisms of the false teachers. The Judaizers relentlessly dogged his steps, plotting at every turn to get rid of him. He suffered so greatly that he literally says, "I die daily" (1 Cor. 15:31). That wasn't some mystical, spiritual experience; what he meant was, "I get up every morning prepared for the reality that this could be the day I die."

So much of his suffering was at the hands of the very people he loved the most. He even said to the Corinthians, "How is it that the more I love you, the less you love me? I don't get it." And yet, he knew that this treatment was commensurate with what he deserved. He even realized that the ill treatment he received kept him dependent on God. He says, "When I am weak, then I am strong" (2 Cor. 12:10).

His defense all the way through is, "You're right; you're right; you're right. I'm weak, I know." He does not argue against the false teachers' accusations of weakness; rather he affirms them. Yet his weaknesses are not defects; they are credentials of his authentic apostleship. This little section in 2 Corinthians 4 unfolds for us a magnificent tribute to a humble man. He defends himself not on the basis of natural talent, human skill, or achievement. He just agrees, and he makes a comparison that is magnificent.

Paul writes, "We have this treasure in earthen vessels, [so] that the surpassing greatness of the power may be of God and not from ourselves" (v. 7). God puts the priceless treasure in clay pots for this very reason: *no one ever has to ask where the power comes from!*

In comparison to the glory of the eternal God revealed in the person of Jesus Christ, in comparison to the magnificence of the New Covenant expressed all through chapter 3, in comparison to Christ's shining glory, the preacher is nothing!

In chapter 10, Paul says, "I don't get into comparing myself with other preachers. I just start here: 'We have this treasure, this ministry.'" The ministry is "the gospel of the glory of Christ, who is the image of God" (4:4). The gospel is the treasure. It is the story of God incarnate in Christ redeeming sinners, that great shining gospel. That is what Paul describes in the wondrous third chapter, where he unfolds the New Covenant. He says the treasure is the truth. It is the truth that God is in Christ, bringing good news of salvation. And He put that treasure in clay pots.

A clay pot is made of baked dirt. It is common, breakable, replaceable, and of little value. If you drop one, it is no big deal. A clay pot is just a clay pot. However, though it may be cheap, it is useful. Clay pots in ancient times were used for a number of tasks. Sometimes something important was put in a clay pot, like the Dead Sea Scrolls. Sometimes they were used to contain semi-valuable things which were then buried in the ground. In the home, however, they were mostly used for garbage and waste—to carry out what was unmentionable.

In 2 Timothy 2:20, the same word for "clay pots" is used, making it clear what we have here: "Now in a large house there are not only gold and silver vessels, but also vessels of wood and of earthenware, and some to honor and some to dishonor." The wood and clay pots held things that were dirty, dishonorable, and perhaps unmentionable. The only value they had was in the service they performed. Paul says in verse 21 that if anyone wants to use any of the wood or clay pots for something honorable, he must cleanse it first because it has been defiled.

So now we can better understand 2 Corinthians 4. Paul is saying, "We have this treasure in a garbage can, a waste bucket." In other words, we are common containers for the most humble and most dirty uses; we are never, ever fit, in and of ourselves, to be brought into public. That's how it is in the ministry. Our only value is as containers. It's the treasure that we bring that has the value. That's why the Lord didn't choose many mighty or noble. He has chosen the humble, the base, and the common. This is the essence of spiritual service.

They accused Paul: "You're weak; you're unimpressive; you're not a good communicator; you're plain; you're common; you're not clever; you're not philosophical; and you're not culturally sensitive."

His response was this: "I know; I know. I'm just a pot—but do I have a treasure!"

The New Testament was not written by the elite of Egypt. It was not written by the elite of Greece, Rome, or even Israel. The greatest scholars in the world at that time were down at Egypt; they were in the greatest library of antiquity at Alexandria. The most distinguished philosophers were in Athens; the most powerful leaders of men were in Rome; and the religious geniuses were in Israel's temple. But God never used any of them! He just used clay pots. He passed by Herodotus, the historian; Socrates, the philosopher; Hippocrates, the father of medicine; Euclid, the mathematician; Archimedes, the father of mechanics; Hipparchus, the astronomer; Cicero, the orator; and Virgil, the poet. He passed by them all. Why? Clay pots served His purposes better. From a human viewpoint (and perhaps in their own minds), all those prominent people were magnificent vessels. But someone deeply impressed with his own value isn't going to see value in the gospel. So God chose peasants, fishermen, smelly guys, and tax collectors—clay pots chosen to carry, proclaim, and write the priceless treasure we call the gospel.

God Uses Clay Pots Today

God is still doing it that way. He is still passing by the elite. He is still passing by the hard-hearted, non-listening, proud intellectuals. They may be sitting in their ivory towers in the universities and seminaries, or in their bishoprics and their positions of authority in the churches, but God is finding the humble who will carry the treasure of saving truth.

How can that work? It works because "we do not preach ourselves" (2 Cor. 4:5). We are not the message. The church I pastor has been blessed because God has blessed His truth. It's not me. When Paul says, "When I am weak, then I am strong," he doesn't mean that he is a man with no convictions. Neither does he mean that he is an undisciplined man, a lazy man, an irresponsible man, or a man who can't work hard. What he means by "weak" is this: "I got myself out of the equation. And that's when the strength became apparent—when I got myself out of the way."

If you want to be used mightily by God, get yourself out of the way. Learn to see yourself as a garbage pail, or, in the words of Peter, to clothe yourself with humility (1 Peter 5:5). It's not about you; it's not your personality, it's the Word of God. God doesn't need the intellectuals. He doesn't need great people, fancy people, or famous people. The people aren't the power. The power is the message!

He puts the treasure in clay pots so that "the surpassing greatness of the power may be of God and not from ourselves" (2 Cor. 4:7b).

If you look for a human explanation for Paul's success, there isn't one. People have said to me, "I'm studying the Bible to see why Paul was successful." I'll tell you why he was successful: he preached the truth. And the truth is powerful. Or they will say, "We want to come to your church to find out what makes things tick there." I'll tell you what makes things tick there: the truth of God. The truth of God and the power of God; those are what make things tick. The surpassing greatness explains the transcendent might of superlative power from God on the souls of those who hear the truth. We preachers are clay pots at best! In and of ourselves, we have nothing to offer, neither beauty nor power. Paul knew that, which is why he says, "I was with you in weakness and in fear and in much trembling" (1 Cor. 2:3b).

In the end, it's OK that we're so weak and so afraid. Our faith should not rest in ourselves anyway, but in the power of God. *We're nothing.* As Paul says elsewhere, "Neither the one who plants nor the one who waters is anything, but God who causes the growth" (1 Cor. 3:7). *God is everything!*

Years ago, James Denney wrote: "No one who saw Paul's ministry and looked at a preacher like Paul could dream that the explanation lay in him. Not in an ugly little Jew without presence, without eloquence, without the means to bribe or to compel could the source of such courage, the cause of such transformation, be found. It must be sought not in him, but in God." In 1911, in his book *The Glory of the Ministry*, A. T. Robertson quoted Denney: "There always have been men in the world so clever that God could make no use of them. They could never do His work; they were so lost in admiration of their own. God's work never depended on them, and it doesn't depend on them now. The power is not the product of human genius, or cleverness, or technique, or ingenuity; the power of the gospel is in the gospel." We ministers are weak, common, plain, fragile, breakable, dishonorable, and disposable clay pots who should be taking the garbage out—but instead we're bringing the glory of God to our people.

The amazing thing is that such weakness does not prove fatal to the gospel. Thankfully, the gospel is not from us. The great reality is, God's clay-pot strategy is essential to the gospel, because it makes crystal clear where the power really lies. We are unworthy servants, but God has given us the treasure of the gospel. What an inestimable privilege!

Endnotes

---

1 This chapter is adapted from a message delivered to pastors at Grace Community Church's annual Shepherd's Conference in 2001.

2 Unless otherwise indicated, all Scripture quotations in this chapter are from the New American Standard Version.